The Power of Your Subconscious Mind

Titles by Joseph Murphy

THE POWER OF YOUR SUBCONSCIOUS MIND
THE MIRACLE OF MIND DYNAMICS
YOUR INFINITE POWER TO BE RICH
SECRETS OF THE I CHING
THE AMAZING LAWS OF COSMIC MIND POWER
THINK YOURSELF RICH
THINK YOURSELF TO HEALTH, WEALTH & HAPPINESS
PUTTING THE POWER OF YOUR SUBCONSCIOUS MIND TO WORK

September 2021
To Annemarie
May you find some
wisdom within these
Pages
Love Kit xx

Enjoy

The Power of Your Subconscious Mind

Joseph Murphy, Ph.D., D.D.
Edited and revised by Arthur R. Pell, Ph.D.

**SIMON &
SCHUSTER**

London · New York · Sydney · Toronto · New Delhi

Original English Language edition published by Prentice Hall Direct
This paperback edition published by Simon & Schuster UK Ltd, 2018

Published by arrangement with TarcherPerigee, an imprint of
Penguin Publishing Group, a division of Penguin Random House LLC.

The only revision authorised by The Murphy Trust

7 9 10 8 6

Simon & Schuster UK Ltd
1st Floor
222 Gray's Inn Road
London WC1X 8HB

www.simonandschuster.co.uk
www.simonandschuster.com.au
www.simonandschuster.co.in

Simon & Schuster Australia, Sydney
Simon & Schuster India, New Delhi

A CIP catalogue record for this book is available from the British Library

Paperback ISBN: 978-1-4711-7939-6

Printed and bound by CPI Group (UK) Ltd, Croydon, CR0 4YY

MIX
Paper from
responsible sources
FSC® C020471

Contents

Introduction

Are You Getting the Most Out of Life?

Life should be an adventure. Life should be fulfilling. Life should be much more than just existing. But most men and women are so bogged down with the day-to-day minutiae of striving to survive that they do not savor the wonders of being alive.

Most people are experiencing only a fraction of the joy and satisfaction that God placed before them. There is a way that each of us can change that and revitalize our lives.

Dr. Murphy was the founder of the Power of the Subconscious Mind movement, which has since been adopted by many philosophers, psychologists, clergy, and writers in many countries. He has helped thousands of men and women change their lives from boring, humdrum, sometimes debilitated existences to vibrant, meaningful, rewarding lives.

In this seminal work, Dr. Murphy combines time-honored spiritual wisdom with solid science-based analyses to explain the influence of the subconscious mind. He also presents simple, practical, and proven-effective exercises that can turn the mind into a powerful tool for improving everyday life. Illustrated with inspiring real-life success stories, this invaluable user's guide to the mind unlocks the secrets to success in a wide range of endeavors including:

- Building self-confidence

- Improving health

- Developing friendships and enhancing existing relationships with coworkers, family, and friends

- Getting that much-wanted promotion, raise, or recognition

- Strengthening marriage and love relationships

- Developing good habits and overcoming bad habits

As Dr. Murphy was a clergyman, he makes frequent reference to the Bible and cites quotations from both the Old and New Testaments. However, he points out that the principles he expounds are not limited to any one faith or religion, but are universally true. His work is founded on the thoughts and concepts of the great prophets, theologians, and philosophers from all religions and nations, both in ancient and modern times. They are applicable to all of today's readers, no matter what their spiritual background may be.

This edition is the only revision of *The Power of Your Subconscious Mind* that has been authorized and published under the auspices of the Murphy Trust, the official custodian of Dr. Murphy's works. In this newly revised edition Dr. Murphy's message is presented in his own words with minor changes to make the book more accessible to readers of the twenty-first century. For instance, the longer Bible verses quoted here are from *The New English Bible* (published by the Oxford University Press, 1970), replacing the original translations from the King James version. In addition to the original material, each chapter includes excerpts drawn from various works, published and unpublished, by Dr. Murphy, to emphasize key points covered.

Read this book with an open mind. Dr. Murphy's precepts are not theoretical. They are based on time-proven concepts supported by examples from real life. Countless people who applied these principles have learned how to make the most out of their lives.

Read. Learn. Apply. You can change your life for the better.

—Arthur R. Pell, Ph.D.

How This Book Can Work Miracles in Your Life

I have seen miracles happen to men and women in all walks of life all over the world. Miracles will happen to you, too—when you begin using the magic power of your subconscious mind. This book is designed to teach you that your habitual thinking and imagery mold, fashion, and create your destiny. For as a person thinks in his subconscious mind, so he is.

Do You Know the Answers?

Why is one person sad and another person happy? Why is one person joyous and prosperous and another person poor and miserable? Why is one person fearful and anxious and another full of faith and confidence? Why does one person have a beautiful, luxurious home while another person lives out a meager existence in a slum?

Why is one person a great success and another an abject

failure? Why is one speaker outstanding and immensely popular and another mediocre and unpopular? Why is one person a genius in her work or profession while another toils and moils all his life without doing or accomplishing anything worthwhile?

Why is one person healed of a so-called incurable disease and another isn't? Why is it that so many good, kind, religious people suffer the tortures of the damned in their minds and bodies? Why is it that many immoral and irreligious people succeed and prosper and enjoy radiant health? Why is one person happily married and another very unhappy and frustrated?

Is there an answer to these questions in the workings of your conscious and subconscious minds?

There most certainly is.

My Reason for Writing This Book

What motivated me to write this book was a deep desire to share with others the answers I have discovered to these and many similar questions. I have tried to explain the great fundamental truths of your mind in the simplest language possible. I believe that it is perfectly possible to explain the basic and fundamental laws of life and of your mind in ordinary everyday language. You will find that the language of this book is the same that's used in your daily papers and current periodicals, in your business offices, in your home, and in the daily workshop.

I urge you to study this book and apply the techniques it outlines. As you do, I'm absolutely convinced that you will lay hold of a miracle-working power that will lift you up from confusion, misery, melancholy, and failure. It will guide you to your true place, solve your difficulties, sever you from emotional and physical bondage, and place you on the royal road to freedom, happiness, and peace of mind.

This miracle-working power of your subconscious mind can

heal you of your sickness, making you vital and strong again. In learning how to use your inner powers, you will open the prison door of fear and enter into a life described as the glorious liberty of the sons of God.

Releasing the Miracle-Working Power

A personal healing will always be the most convincing evidence of our subconscious powers. Many years ago I managed to cure myself of a malignancy—in medical terminology it is called a sarcoma—by using the healing power of my subconscious mind, which created me and still maintains and governs all my vital functions.

The technique I applied then is explained in detail in this book. I feel sure that it will help others to trust the same Infinite Healing Presence lodged in the subconscious depths of all of us. Thanks to the kindly advice of an elderly doctor friend, I suddenly realized that it is natural to assume that the creative intelligence that made all my organs, fashioned my body, and started my heart can heal its own handiwork. As the ancient proverb says, "The doctor dresses the wound and God heals it."

Wonders Happen When You Pray Effectively

Scientific prayer is the harmonious interaction of the conscious and subconscious levels of mind scientifically directed toward a specific purpose. This book will teach you the scientific way to tap the realm of Infinite Power within you, enabling you to get what you really want in life. You desire a happier, fuller, and richer life. Begin to use this miracle-working power and smooth your way in daily affairs, solve business problems, and bring harmony in family relationships.

Be sure that you read this book several times. You will discover how this wonderful power works and how you can draw out the hidden inspiration and wisdom that is within you. Learn the simple techniques of impressing the subconscious mind. Follow the new scientific way in tapping the infinite storehouse. Read this book carefully, earnestly, and lovingly. Prove to yourself the amazing way it can help you. It may be—and I believe it will be—the turning point of your life.

Everybody Prays

Do you know how to pray effectively? How long has it been since you prayed as part of your everyday activities? In an emergency, in time of danger or trouble, in illness, and when death lurks, prayers pour forth.

Just listen to the TV news each day. There are reports that people all over the world are praying for a child stricken with a so-called incurable ailment, for peace among nations, for a group of miners trapped in a flooded mine. Later we hear that when rescued, the miners say they prayed while waiting for rescue.

Certainly, prayer is an ever-present help in time of trouble. But why should you wait for trouble to make prayer an integral and constructive part of your life? The dramatic answers to prayer make headlines and are the subject of testimonies to the effectiveness of prayer. But what of the many humble prayers of children, the simple thanksgiving of grace at the table daily, the faithful devotions wherein the individual seeks only communion with God?

My work with people has led me to study the various approaches to prayer. I have experienced the power of prayer in my own life, and I have talked and worked with many others who have benefited greatly from the help of prayer. The problem usually is how to tell someone else how to pray. People who are in trouble have difficulty in thinking and acting reasonably. Their problems overwhelm them and block their ability to listen and understand. They need an *easy* formula to follow, an obviously workable pattern that is simple and specific.

Everyday Prayer

The unique feature of this book is its down-to-earth practicality. Here you will find simple, usable techniques and formulas that you can easily apply in your everyday life. I have taught these simple processes to men and women all over the world.

You will learn why you often get the opposite of what you prayed for. Thousands of times, people in all parts of the world have asked me, "Why is it I have prayed and prayed and got no answer?" In this book you will find the reasons for this common complaint. The explanation of the many ways of impressing the subconscious mind and getting the right answers make this an extraordinarily valuable book and an ever-present help in times of trouble.

What Do You Believe?

Contrary to what many people think, it is not the thing that is believed in that brings an answer to a person's prayer. Prayers are answered when the individual's subconscious mind responds to the mental picture or thought in his or her mind. This law of belief is the secret operating principle in all the religions of the world. It is the hidden reason for their psychological truth.

The Buddhist, the Christian, the Moslem, and the Jew may all get answers to their prayers, in spite of the enormous differences among their stated beliefs. How can this be? The answer is that it is not because of the particular creed, religion, affiliation, ritual, ceremony, formula, liturgy, incantation, sacrifices, or offerings, but solely because of belief or mental acceptance and receptivity about that for which they pray.

The law of life is the law of belief. Belief can be summed up briefly as a thought in your mind. As a person thinks, feels, and believes, so is the condition of his or her mind, body, and circumstances. A technique, a methodology based on an understanding of what you are doing and why you are doing it will help you to bring about a subconscious embodiment of all the good things of life. Essentially, answered prayer is the realization of your heart's desire.

Desire Is Prayer

Everyone desires health, happiness, security, peace of mind, and true expression. But how many of us achieve all these goals? A university professor admitted to me recently, "I know that if I change my mental pattern and redirect my emotional life, my heart condition will improve. I *know* that. The problem is, I do not have any technique, process, or modus operandi. My mind wanders back and forth on my many problems, and I feel frustrated, unhappy, and defeated."

This professor had the *desire* for perfect health. What he needed was knowledge of the way his mind worked. It was this that would enable him to fulfill his desire. By practicing the healing methods outlined in this book, he became whole and perfect.

Time Is One Mind Common to All Individuals

The miracle-working powers of your subconscious mind existed before you and I were born, before any church or world existed. The great eternal truths and principles of life antedate all religions. It is with these thoughts in mind that I urge you in the following chapters to lay hold of this wonderful, magical, transforming power. It will bind up mental and physical wounds, proclaim liberty to the fear-ridden mind, and liberate you completely from the limitations of poverty, failure, misery, lack, and frustration.

All you have to do is unite mentally and emotionally with the good you wish to embody. The creative powers of your subconscious will respond accordingly. Begin now, today. Let wonders happen in your life! Keep on keeping on until the day breaks and the shadows flee away.

Your Subconscious Mind Is a Darkroom

Your subconscious is your great darkroom. It's the secret place where your outer life develops.

Therefore it isn't your name, your manner of dress, your parents, your neighborhood, or the automobile you drive that makes you what and who you are. You are the beliefs taking shape, image by image, light and shadow, there in your subterranean darkroom. In a moral sense, your subconscious is totally neutral, willing to look on any habit as fitting, whether or not you or the world deems it good or bad. That is why when we blithely drop negative thoughts into our subconscious, into this darkroom of ours, time and time again, we are so surprised to see these dark thoughts finding expression in our day-to-day experiences and relationships . . . time and time again. As a matter of fact, it is rare to find something happening to us that we had no role in creating in this way.

In order for your world to change, you have to change your mind . . . from the inside out. But if you accept this darkroom concept you will find yourself happily free of emotion about the process. When you entertain this idea, you will find that changing your life won't be such a struggle. How much of an effort can it take to simply replace existing mental images with new ones? This understanding can mean the beginning of an easeful period of positive change for you.

It may surprise you to learn that all the beliefs and tendencies that were instilled in you from your earliest days are still with you, and they have power to manifest in and influence your life. All of us have many such beliefs and ideas that we have long since forgotten about, beliefs and ideas that perhaps had their origins in childhood. These are hidden in the deeper recesses of this subconscious darkroom. Knowing this should make it clear why it's time to develop a healthy respect for your thoughts.

For example, if you believe that sitting near a fan will give you a stiff neck, your subconscious mind will see to it that you get a stiff neck. It is not the action of the fan, which represents innocuous molecules of energy oscillating at a high frequency, that will cause your discomfort, but your erroneous beliefs. The fan is harmless.

And if you're afraid that you'll catch a cold because someone in the office sneezes, your fear becomes a movement of your own mind that creates what you expect, what you fear and believe. You'll notice that others in the office don't get a cold because they don't believe in it. They believe in health.

Job said, *What I greatly feared has come upon me.*

On the other hand, where do you think miraculous healing power also comes from? From the same subconscious mind . . . If you fill your darkroom with great truths, your outer pictures will reflect them. Your subconscious mind will accept these truths and you will be under a subconscious compulsion to heal, to be peaceful. Just as an apple becomes your bloodstream, do these thoughts reside in your mind and affect your life. It is the same way you learned to walk, swim, dance, or play the piano. You repeat a thought again and again, and after awhile it becomes second nature. That's prayer, that's conforming to a higher principle. The gasoline doesn't run your car. It has to become a vapor first, it has to change before it becomes empowered, just as your mind has to change before your world moves to where you want it.

Along with healing, your subconscious darkroom is where your wealth is produced. The key is to first make the subconscious rich before you can see abundance in your life.

As you become a student of the laws of mind, you will come to believe and know definitely that regardless of economic situations, stock market fluctuation, depression, strikes, war, or other conditions or circumstances, you will always be amply supplied. The reason for this is that you will have conveyed the idea of wealth to your subconscious mind, will have supplied your darkroom with an image of wealth, and you *will* be supplied. You will have convinced your secret mind that money is forever flowing freely in your life and that there is always a wonderful surplus. Should there be a financial collapse of government tomorrow and all your present holdings become valueless, you would still attract wealth and be cared for.

Your subconscious darkroom is filled with great new ideas, so you don't have to worry about replacing your old ones. Begin at once to think about whatever things are true, lovely, and noble, and you will see these qualities around you. Remember that God pronounced everything good and very good, and so should you. Thinking this way will give you a new, healthy reverence for your thoughts, and you will find that you will no longer be a victim of pictures you thought you had no part in developing.

Chapter One

The Treasure House Within You

The tendency of your subconscious mind is always lifeward. Your job is with the conscious mind. Feed your conscious mind with the premises that are true. Your subconscious is always reproducing according to your habitual mental patterns.

You have infinite riches within your reach. To gain them, all you have to do is open your mental eyes and behold the treasure house of Infinity within you. There is a storehouse within you from which you can extract everything you need to live life gloriously, joyously, and abundantly.

Many people are closed off to their own potential because they do not know about this storehouse of Infinite Intelligence and boundless love within themselves. Whatever you want, you can draw it forth.

A magnetized piece of iron will lift about twelve times its own weight. But if you demagnetize this same piece of iron, it will not lift even a feather.

In the same way, there are two types of people. Those who are magnetized are full of confidence and faith. They know they are born to succeed and to win.

Others—so many others—are demagnetized. They are full of fears and doubts. When an opportunity comes, they say, "What if I fail? I might lose my money. People will laugh at me." People of this sort will not get very far in life. Their fear to go forward makes them simply stay where they are.

You can become a magnetized person when you discover and put to use the master secret of the ages.

The Master Secret of the Ages

Suppose someone asked you to name the master secret of the ages. What would you answer? Atomic energy? Interplanetary travel? Black holes? No, it is not any of these. Then what is this master secret? Where can one find it? How can it be understood and put into action?

The answer is extraordinarily simple. This secret is the marvelous, miracle-working power found in your own subconscious mind. This is the last place most people would look for it, which is the reason so few ever find it.

The Marvelous Power of Your Subconscious

Once you learn to contact and release the hidden power of your subconscious mind, you can bring into your life more power, more wealth, more health, more happiness, and more joy.

You do not need to acquire this power. You already possess it. But you will have to learn how to use it. You must understand it so that you can apply it in all departments of your life.

If you follow the simple techniques and processes explained in this book, you can gain the necessary knowledge and understanding. You can be inspired by a new light, and you can generate a new force that enables you to realize your hopes and make all your dreams come true. Decide now to make your life grander, greater, richer, and nobler than ever before.

Within your subconscious depths lie Infinite Wisdom, Infinite Power, an infinite supply of all that is necessary. It is waiting there for you to give it development and expression. If you begin now to recognize these potentialities of your deeper mind, they will take form in the world without.

Provided you are open-minded and receptive, the Infinite Intelligence within your subconscious mind can reveal to you everything you need to know at every moment of time and point of space. You can receive new thoughts and ideas, bring forth new inventions, make new discoveries, create new works of art. The Infinite Intelligence in your subconscious can give you access to wonderful new kinds of knowledge. Let it reveal itself to you and it will open the way to perfect expression and true place in your life.

Through the wisdom of your subconscious mind, you can attract the ideal companion, as well as the right business associate or partner. It can show you how to get all the money you need and give you the financial freedom to be, to do, and to go as your heart desires.

It is your right to discover this inner world of thought, feeling, and power, of light, love, and beauty. Though invisible, its forces are mighty. Within your subconscious mind you will find the solution for every problem and the cause for every effect. Once you learn to draw out these hidden powers, you come into actual possession of the power and wisdom necessary to move forward in abundance, security, joy, and dominion.

I have seen the power of the subconscious lift people up out of crippled states, making them whole, vital, and strong once more. Their minds made them free to go out into the world to experience happiness, health, and joyous expression. There is a miraculous curative force in your subconscious that can heal the troubled mind and the broken heart. It can open the prison door of the mind and liberate you. It can free you from all kinds of material and physical bondage.

Find a Working Basis

If you want to make progress in any field of endeavor, there is an essential first step. You must discover a working basis that is universal in its application. Before you can become skilled in the operation of your subconscious mind, you must understand its principles. Once that is achieved, you can practice its powers knowing the results you will certainly obtain. You can apply these powers for the definite specific purposes and goals you want to accomplish.

For many years I followed the profession of chemist. One of the first things I learned in my early training was that if you combine two atoms of hydrogen and one of oxygen, the product will be water—not occasionally or most of the time, *always*. If you take one atom of oxygen and one atom of carbon and combine them, you will produce carbon monoxide, a poisonous gas. But if you add another atom of oxygen, you will get carbon dioxide, a gas that is harmless to animals and vital to plants. These facts are universal and unchangeable. They are what we call principles.

The principles of chemistry, physics, and mathematics are no different in their workings from the principles of your subconscious mind. If you want to make use of chemical or physical forces, you must learn the principles of these fields. If you want to make use of the force of your subconscious mind, you must learn its principles.

Take the generally accepted principle *water seeks its own level*. This is a universal principle. It applies to water everywhere, at any time, and to all liquids that behave like water.

The ancient Egyptians knew this principle. They used it to make the foundations of the great pyramids perfectly level.

Today, engineers use it when planning everything from an irrigation system to a hydroelectric power station.

Or take the principle *matter expands when heated*. This is true anywhere, at any time, and under all circumstances. If you heat a piece of steel, it will expand, whether the steel is found in China, England, India, or in an orbiting space station.

Matter expands when heated. This is a universal truth. It is also a universal truth that whatever you impress on your subconscious mind is expressed on the screen of space as condition, experience, and event.

Your prayer is answered because your subconscious mind is principle, and by principle I mean the way a thing works. For example, an important principle of electricity is that it works from a higher to a lower potential. You do not change the principle of electricity when you turn on a lamp or cook on an electric stove. No, you *use* the principle. By cooperating with nature, you can bring forth marvelous inventions and discoveries that bless humanity in countless ways.

Your subconscious mind is principle. It works according to the law of belief. You must know what belief is, why it works, and how it works. The Bible says in a simple, clear, and beautiful way:

> *If anyone says to this mountain "Be lifted from your place and hurled into the sea," and has no inward doubts, but believes that what he says is happening, it will be done for him. I tell you, then, whatever you ask for in prayer, believe that you have received it and it will be yours.* (Mark 11:23–24)

The law of your mind is the law of belief. This means to believe in the way your mind works, to believe in belief itself. The belief of your mind is the thought of your mind, just that and nothing else.

All your experiences, events, conditions, and acts are produced by your subconscious mind in reaction to your thoughts. Remember, it is not the thing believed in, but the belief in your own mind that brings about the result. Stop accepting the false beliefs, opinions, superstitions, and fears that plague our humankind. Begin to believe in the eternal verities and truths of life that never change. At that point you will move onward, upward, and Godward.

All those who read this book and faithfully apply the principles of the subconscious mind that are set forth here will gain the ability to pray scientifically and effectively for themselves and for others. Your prayer is answered according to the universal law of *action and reaction*. Thought is incipient action. The reaction is the response from your subconscious mind that corresponds to the nature of your thought. Fill your mind with the concepts of harmony, health, peace, and goodwill, and wonders will happen in your life.

Whether the object of your faith is real or false, you will get results. Your subconscious mind responds to the thought in your mind. Look upon faith as a thought in your mind and that will suffice.

Know that you can remake yourself by giving a new blueprint to your subconscious mind.

The Duality of Mind

You have only one mind, but that one mind possesses two distinct and characteristic functional parts. The frontier that separates the two is well known to students of the mind. The two functions of your mind are essentially different from each other. Each has its own separate and distinct attributes and powers.

Many names have been used to distinguish the two functions of the mind. These include the objective and the subjective mind, the conscious and the subconscious mind, the waking and the sleeping mind, the surface and the deep self, the voluntary and the involuntary mind, the male and the female mind, and many others. All of these, whatever their implications, are recognitions of this essential duality.

Throughout this book I use the terms *conscious* and *subconscious* to represent the dual nature of your mind. If another set of terms comes more easily to you, by all means use it. The important starting point is to recognize and acknowledge the double nature of the mind.

The Conscious and the Subconscious Minds

A wonderful way to begin getting to know the two functions of your mind is to think of it as a garden. You are the gardener. You are planting seeds of thought in your subconscious mind all day long. Much of the time you are not even aware of doing so, because the seeds are based on your habitual thinking. As you sow in your subconscious mind, so shall you reap in your body and environment.

Imagine your subconscious mind as a bed of rich soil that will help all kinds of seeds to sprout and flourish, whether good or bad. If you sow thorns, will you gather grapes? If you sow thistles, will you harvest figs? Every thought is a cause, and every condition is an effect. This is the reason it is so essential that you take charge of your thoughts. In that way, you can bring forth only desirable conditions.

Begin now to sow thoughts of peace, happiness, right action, goodwill, and prosperity. Think quietly and with conviction on these qualities. Accept them fully in your conscious reasoning mind. Continue to plant these wonderful seeds of thought in the garden of your mind and you will reap a glorious harvest.

When your mind thinks correctly, when you understand the truth, when the thoughts deposited in your subconscious mind are constructive, harmonious, and peaceful, the magic working power of your subconscious will respond. It will bring about harmonious conditions, agreeable surroundings, and the best of everything. Once you begin to control your thought processes, you can apply the powers of your subconscious to any problem or difficulty. You will actually be consciously cooperating with the Infinite Power and omnipotent law that governs all things.

Look around you. Wherever you live, whatever circle of society you are part of, you will notice that most people live in the world "without." Those who are more enlightened, however, are intensely involved with the world "within." They realize—as you will, too—that the world within *creates* the world without. Your thoughts, feelings, and visualized imagery are the organizing principles of your experience. The world within is the only creative power. Everything you find in your world of expression has been created by you in the inner world of your mind, whether consciously or unconsciously.

Once you learn the truth about the interaction of your conscious and subconscious minds, you will be able to transform your whole life. If you want to change external conditions, you must change the cause. Most people try to change conditions and circumstances by working on those conditions and circumstances. This is a terrible waste of time and effort. They fail to see that their conditions flow from a cause. To remove discord, confusion, lack, and limitation from your life, you must remove the cause. That cause is the way you use your conscious mind, the thoughts and images you encourage in it.

Change the cause, and you change the effect. It is just that simple.

We all live in an unfathomable sea of infinite riches. Your subconscious is very sensitive to your conscious thoughts. Those conscious thoughts form the matrix through which the Infinite Intelligence, Wisdom, vital forces, and energies of your subconscious flow. Shape that matrix in a more positive direction and you redirect those infinite energies to your greater benefit.

Each chapter of this book gives concrete, specific illustrations of how to apply the laws of mind. Once you learn to use these techniques, you will experience abundance instead of poverty, wisdom instead of superstition and ignorance, peace instead of inner strife, success instead of failure, joy instead of sadness, light instead of darkness, harmony instead of discord, faith and confidence instead of fear. Could there be any more wonderful set of blessings than these?

Most of the great scientists, artists, poets, singers, writers, and inventors have had a deep understanding of the workings of the conscious and subconscious minds. It was this that gave them the power to accomplish their goals.

The great operatic tenor Enrico Caruso was once struck with stage fright. Spasms caused by intense fear constricted the muscles of his throat. His vocal cords felt paralyzed, useless. He stood backstage, already in costume, while perspiration poured down his face. In just moments he was supposed to go out on the stage and sing before an eager audience of thousands.

Trembling, he said, "I can't sing. They will all laugh at me. My career is finished." He turned to go back to his dressing room. Then, suddenly, he stopped and shouted, "The Little Me is trying to strangle the Big Me within!"

He turned toward the stage again and stood taller. "Get out

of here," he commanded, addressing the Little Me. "The Big Me wants to sing through me."

By the "Big Me," Caruso meant the limitless power and wisdom of his subconscious mind. He began to shout, "Get out, get out, the Big Me is going to sing!" His subconscious mind responded by releasing the vital forces within him. When the call came, he walked out onstage and sang gloriously and majestically. The audience was enthralled.

From what you have already learned, you can see that Caruso understood the two levels of mind—the conscious or rational, and the subconscious or irrational level. Your subconscious mind is reactive. It responds to the nature of your thoughts. When your conscious mind (Caruso's "Little Me") is full of fear, worry, and anxiety, the negative emotions these create in your subconscious mind (the "Big Me") are released. They flood the conscious mind with a sense of panic, foreboding, and despair. When this happens to you, you can follow the example of the great Caruso. You can speak affirmatively and with a deep sense of authority to the irrational emotions generated in your deeper mind. You can say, "Be still. Be quiet. I am in control. You must obey me. You are subject to my command. You cannot intrude where you do not belong."

You will be fascinated to see what happens when you speak authoritatively and with conviction to the irrational movement of your deeper self. Your mind will be flooded with harmony and with peace. The subconscious is *subject* to the conscious mind. That is why it is called subconscious or *subjective*.

Outstanding Differences and Modes of Operation

The conscious mind is like the navigator or captain at the bridge of a ship. He directs the ship. He sends orders to the crew in the engine room. They in turn control the boilers, instruments, gauges, and so on. The people in the engine room do not know where they are going; they follow orders. They would go on the rocks if the man on the bridge issued faulty or wrong instructions based on his findings with the compass, sextant, and other instruments. The people in the engine room obey him because he is in charge. Because he is supposed to know what he is doing, the members of the crew do not talk back to the captain; they simply carry out his orders.

The captain is the master of his ship, and his decrees are carried out. In the same way, your conscious mind is the captain and the master of your ship—your body, your environment, and all your affairs. Your subconscious mind takes the orders you give it, based upon what your conscious mind believes and accepts as true. It does not question the orders or the basis on which they are given.

If you repeatedly say to yourself, "I can't afford it," your subconscious mind takes you at your word. It sees to it that you will not be in a position to buy what you want. As long as you go on saying, "I can't afford that car, that vacation, that home," you can be sure your subconscious mind will follow your orders. You will go through life experiencing the lack of all these things, and you will believe that circumstances made it so. It will not occur to you that you have created those circumstances yourself, by your own negative, denying thoughts.

One Christmas Eve, a young woman named Nina W., who is a student at the University of Southern California, strolled through an exclusive shopping area in Beverly Hills. Her mind was filled with anticipation. She was about to spend the holidays with her family in Buffalo, New York.

As Nina passed a shop window, a beautiful Spanish leather shoulder bag caught her eye. She looked at it yearningly. Then she noticed the price tag and gasped.

She was about to say to herself, "I could never afford such an expensive bag." Then she remembered something she had heard me say at one of my lectures. "Never finish a negative statement. Reverse it immediately and wonders will happen in your life."

Staring through the glass, she said, "That bag is mine. It is for sale. I accept it mentally, and my subconscious sees to it that I receive it."

Later that day, Nina met her fiancé for a send-off dinner. He arrived with an elegantly wrapped gift under his arm. Holding her breath, she unwrapped it. There was the identical leather shoulder bag she had looked at and identified as her own that same morning. She had filled her mind with the thought of expectancy. Then she had turned the matter over to her deeper mind, which has the power of accomplishment.

Later, Nina told me, "I didn't have the money to buy that bag, yet now it is mine. I have learned where to find money and all the things I need, and that is in the treasure house of eternity within me."

How Her Subconscious Responded

I received a letter from a woman named Ruth A. who had attended my lectures. She wrote:

I am seventy-five years old, a widow with a grown family. I was living alone, on a small pension and Social Security. My life seemed barren, hopeless. Then I remembered your lecture about the powers of the subconscious mind. You said that ideas could be conveyed to the subconscious mind by repetition, faith, and expectancy. Could it be true? I decided to try. I had nothing to lose.

I began to repeat frequently, with all the feeling I could muster, "I am wanted. I am loved. I am happily

*married to a kind, loving, and spiritual-minded man. I
am secure and fulfilled."*

*I kept on doing this many times a day for about two
weeks. One day at the corner drugstore, I was introduced to a retired pharmacist. I found him to be kind,
understanding, and very religious. He was a perfect answer to my prayer. Within a week he proposed to me.
Now we are on our honeymoon in Europe. I know that
the intelligence within my subconscious mind brought us
together in divine order.*

Ruth discovered that the treasure house was within her. Her
prayer was felt as true in her heart, and her affirmation sank
down by osmosis into her subconscious mind, which is the creative medium. The moment she succeeded in bringing about a
subjective embodiment, her subconscious mind brought about
the answer through the law of attraction. Her deeper mind, full
of wisdom and intelligence, brought her and her new husband
together in divine order.

Be sure that you think on this:

*All that is true, all that is noble, all that is just and pure,
all that is lovable and gracious, whatever is excellent
and admirable—fill all your thoughts with these things.*
(Philippians 4:8)

IDEAS TO REMEMBER

1. The treasure house is within you. Look within for the
   answer to your heart's desire.

2. The great secret possessed by the great men of all ages
   was their ability to contact and release the powers of
   their subconscious mind. You can do the same.

3. Your subconscious has the answer to all problems. If you suggest to your subconscious prior to sleep, "I want to get up at 6:00 a.m.," it will awaken you at that exact time.

4. Your subconscious mind is the builder of your body and can heal you. Lull yourself to sleep every night with the idea of perfect health, and your subconscious, being your faithful servant, will obey you.

5. Every thought is a cause, and every condition is an effect.

6. If you want to write a book, write a wonderful play, give a better talk to your audience, convey the idea lovingly and feelingly to your subconscious mind and it will respond accordingly.

7. You are like a captain navigating a ship. He or she must give the right orders, or the ship is wrecked. In the same way, you must give the right orders (thoughts and images) to your subconscious mind, which controls and governs all your experiences.

8. Never use such expressions as "I can't afford it" or "I can't do this." Your subconscious mind takes you at your word. It sees to it that you do not have the money or the ability to do what you want to do. Affirm, "I can do all things through the power of my subconscious mind."

9. The law of life is the law of belief. A belief is a thought in your mind. Do not believe in things that will harm or hurt you. Believe in the power of your subconscious to

heal, inspire, strengthen, and prosper you. According to your belief is it done unto you.

10. Change your thoughts, and you change your destiny.

You are the captain of your soul (subconscious mind) and the master of your fate. Remember, you have the capacity to choose. Choose life! Choose health! Choose happiness!

Chapter Two

How Your Mind Works

Whatever your conscious mind assumes and believes to be true, your subconscious mind will accept and bring to pass. Believe in good fortune, divine guidance, right action, and all the blessings of life.

Your mind is your most precious possession. It is always with you, but its most amazing powers will be yours only when you have learned how to use it. As we have seen, there are two levels to your mind—the conscious or rational level and the subconscious or irrational level. You think with your conscious mind, and whatever you habitually think sinks down into your subconscious mind, which then creates according to the nature of your thoughts. Your subconscious mind is the seat of your emotions. It is the creative mind. If you think good, good will follow; if you think evil, evil will follow. This is the way your mind works.

The most important point to remember is this: Once the subconscious mind accepts an idea, it begins to execute it. It is an astonishing and subtle truth that the law of the subconscious mind works for good and bad ideas alike. This law, when applied in a negative way, is the cause of failure, frustration, and unhappiness. When your habitual thinking is harmonious and constructive, however, you experience perfect health, success, and prosperity.

Peace of mind and a healthy body are inevitable once you begin to think and feel in the right way. Whatever you claim mentally and feel as true, your subconscious mind will accept and bring forth into your experience. All you have to do is get your subconscious mind to accept your idea. Once that happens, the law of your subconscious mind will bring forth the health, peace, and prosperity you desire. You give the command or decree, and your subconscious will faithfully reproduce the idea impressed upon it.

The law of your mind is this: The reaction or response you get from your subconscious mind will be determined by the nature of the thought or idea you hold in your conscious mind.

Psychologists and psychiatrists point out that when thoughts are conveyed to your subconscious mind, impressions are made in the brain cells. As soon as your subconscious accepts any idea, it proceeds to put it into effect immediately. Working by association of ideas, it uses every bit of knowledge that you have gathered in your lifetime to bring about its purpose. It draws on the Infinite Power, Energy, and Wisdom within you. It lines up all the laws of nature to get its way. Sometimes it seems to bring about an immediate solution to your difficulties, but at other times it may take days, weeks, or longer. *Its ways are past finding out.*

The Difference Between Conscious and Subconscious

You must remember that the conscious and subconscious are not two minds. They are merely two spheres of activity within one mind. Your conscious mind is the reasoning mind. It is that phase of mind that chooses. For example, you choose your books, your home, and your partner in life. You make all your decisions with your conscious mind. On the other hand, without any conscious choice on your part, your heart is kept functioning automatically, and the vital functions of digestion, circulation, and breathing are carried on by your subconscious mind through processes independent of your conscious control.

Your subconscious mind accepts what is impressed upon it or what you consciously believe. It does not reason things out as your conscious mind does, and it does not argue with you controversially. Your subconscious mind is like a bed of soil that accepts any kind of seed, good or bad. Your thoughts are active; they are the seeds. Negative, destructive thoughts continue to work negatively in your subconscious mind. Sooner or later, they will emerge and take shape as an outer experience that corresponds to their content.

Remember, your subconscious mind does not engage in proving whether your thoughts are good or bad, true or false. It responds according to the nature of your thoughts or suggestions. For example, if you consciously assume that something is true, even though it may be false, your subconscious mind will accept it as true and proceed to bring about results that must necessarily follow *because* you consciously assumed it to be true.

Experiments by Psychologists

Psychologists and others have performed countless experiments on people who are in a hypnotic trance. This research shows clearly that the subconscious mind does not make the selections and comparisons that are necessary for a reasoning process. Your subconscious mind will accept any suggestions, however false. Having once accepted any suggestion, it responds according to the nature of the suggestion given.

To illustrate how suggestible your subconscious mind is, if a practiced hypnotist suggests to one of her subjects that she is Napoleon Bonaparte, or even a cat or a dog, the subject will act out the part with inimitable accuracy. Her personality becomes changed for the time being. She believes herself to be whatever the operator tells her she is.

A skilled hypnotist may suggest to one of his students in the hypnotic state that her back itches, to another that his nose is bleeding, to another that she is a marble statue, to another that she is freezing and the temperature is below zero. Each one will follow out the line of his particular suggestion, totally oblivious to all those surroundings that do not pertain to the hypnotic suggestion.

These simple illustrations portray the difference between your conscious, reasoning mind and your subconscious mind, which is impersonal, nonselective, and accepts as true whatever your conscious mind believes to be true. Hence the importance of selecting thoughts, ideas, and premises that bless, heal, inspire, and fill your soul with joy.

The Terms *Subjective* and *Objective Mind* Clarified

Your conscious mind is sometimes referred to as your *objective mind* because it deals with outward objects. The objective mind is aware of the objective world. Its media of observation are your five physical senses. Your objective mind is your guide and director in your contact with your environment. You gain knowledge through your five senses. Your objective mind learns through observation, experience, and education. As previously pointed out, the greatest function of the objective mind is that of reasoning.

Suppose you are one of the hundreds of thousands of tourists who visits the Grand Canyon every year. You would come to the conclusion that it is one of the world's most amazing natural wonders. This conclusion would be based on your observation of its incredible depth, the complex shaping of the rock formations, the beautiful play of colors among the different geological strata. This is the working of your objective mind.

Your subconscious mind is often referred to as your *subjective mind*. Your subjective mind is aware of its environment, but not by means of the physical senses. Your subjective mind perceives by intuition. It is the seat of your emotions and the storehouse of memory. Your subjective mind performs its highest functions when your objective senses are not functioning. In other words, it is that intelligence that makes itself known when the objective mind is suspended or in a sleepy, drowsy state.

Your subjective mind sees without the use of the natural organs of vision. It has the capacity of clairvoyance and clairaudience: It can see and hear events that are taking place elsewhere. Your subjective mind can leave your body, travel to distant lands, and bring back information that is often of the most exact and truthful character. Through your subjective mind you can read the thoughts of others, read the contents of sealed envelopes, or intuit the information on a computer disk without using a disk drive.

Once we understand the interaction of the objective and subjective minds, we are in a better position to learn the true art of prayer.

The Subconscious Cannot Reason Like Your Conscious Mind

Your subconscious mind does not have the ability to argue or dispute what it is told. If you give it wrong information, it will accept it as true. It will then work to make that information correct. It will bring your suggestions, *even those that were false,* to pass as conditions, experiences, and events.

Everything that has happened to you happened because of thoughts impressed on your subconscious mind through belief. If you have communicated wrong or distorted concepts to your subconscious mind, it is of the most urgent importance to correct them. The sure way to do this is by repeatedly giving your subconscious mind constructive, harmonious thoughts. As these are frequently repeated, your subconscious mind accepts them. In this way, you can form new, healthier habits of thought and life, for your subconscious mind is the seat of habit.

The habitual thinking of your conscious mind establishes deep grooves in your subconscious mind. If your habitual thoughts are harmonious, peaceful, and constructive, your subconscious mind will respond by creating harmony, peace, and constructive conditions.

Have you fallen prey to fear, worry, and other destructive forms of thinking? The remedy is to recognize the power of your subconscious mind and decree freedom, happiness, and perfect health. Your subconscious mind, being creative and one with your divine source, will then start to create the freedom and happiness you have earnestly decreed.

The Tremendous Power of Suggestion

As you can see by what we have already discussed, your conscious mind serves as the "watchman at the gate." One of its most crucial functions is to protect your subconscious mind from false impressions. The reason this is so important goes back to one of the basic laws of mind: Your subconscious mind is very sensitive to suggestion.

As you know, your subconscious mind does not make

comparisons or contrasts. It doesn't reason and think things out for itself. This latter function belongs to your conscious mind. No, your subconscious mind simply reacts to the impressions given to it by your conscious mind. It does not pick and choose among different courses of action. It merely takes what it is given.

Suggestion is a tremendously powerful force. Imagine that you are on board a ship that is rocking a bit from side to side. You approach a timid-looking fellow passenger and say, "Gee, you don't look so hot. Your face is practically green! I'm afraid you're about to be seasick. Can I help you to your cabin?"

The passenger turns pale. The suggestion you have just made about seasickness links up with her own fears and forebodings. She lets you escort her down belowdecks. Once she is there, your negative suggestion, which she accepted, comes true.

Different Reactions to the Same Suggestion

It is important to realize that different people will react in different ways to the same suggestion. This is because they have different subconscious conditioning or beliefs.

Suppose, instead of choosing a fellow passenger on the ship, you go up to a member of the crew. You say, "Hey, buddy, you don't look so great. Do you think you're about to be seasick?"

Depending on the sailor's temperament, he either laughs at your feeble joke or tells you to get lost. Your suggestion had no power over him, because the idea of seasickness was associated in his mind with his own immunity from it. Therefore, it called up not fear or worry, but self-confidence.

A dictionary will tell you that a suggestion is the act or instance of putting something into one's mind. It is the mental process by which the thought or idea that has been suggested is entertained, accepted, or put into effect. Remember, a suggestion cannot impose itself on the subconscious mind against the will of the conscious mind. Your conscious mind has the power to reject the suggestion.

The sailor had no fear of seasickness. He had convinced himself of his immunity, so the negative suggestion had no power to evoke fear. But your fellow passenger was already worried about becoming sick. Therefore your suggestion had power over her.

All of us have our own inner fears, beliefs, and opinions. These inner assumptions rule and govern our lives. A suggestion has no power in and of itself. Its power arises from the fact that you accept it mentally. Only at that point do your subconscious powers begin to act according to the nature of the suggestion.

How He Lost His Arm

For many years I gave a regular series of lectures at the London Truth Forum in Caxton Hall, which I founded. Dr. Evelyn Fleet, the director, told me about a man whose young daughter suffered from both crippling rheumatoid arthritis and the disfiguring and painful skin condition called psoriasis. They tried many treatments, but nothing the doctors did seemed to help. The man was near despair. Over and over he said, to himself and to his friends, "I would give my right arm to see my daughter cured."

According to Dr. Fleet, one day the family was out for a drive. Their car was involved in a head-on collision. The father's right arm was torn off at the shoulder. When he came home from the hospital, he discovered that his daughter's arthritis and skin condition had vanished.

You must be very careful to give your subconscious only those suggestions that heal, bless, elevate, and inspire you in all your ways. Remember, your subconscious mind doesn't understand a joke. It takes you at your word.

How Autosuggestion Banishes Fear

The term *autosuggestion* means suggesting something definite and specific to oneself. Like any tool, wrongly used it can cause harm, but used properly it can be extremely helpful.

Janet R. was a talented young singer. She was invited to try out for an important role in an opera production. She desperately wanted to audition, but she was also terribly apprehensive.

Three times before, when she had sung for directors, she had failed miserably. The reason was fear of failure. She had a wonderful voice, but she had been saying to herself, "When the time comes for me to sing, I'll sound awful. I'll never get the role. They won't like me. They'll wonder how I have the nerve even to try out. I'll go, but I know it'll be a failure."

Her subconscious mind accepted these negative autosuggestions as a request. It proceeded to manifest them and bring them into her experience. The cause was an involuntary autosuggestion. Her fears had become emotionalized and subjectified thoughts that in turn became her reality.

This young singer was able to overcome the force of her negative autosuggestions. She accomplished this by countering them with *positive* autosuggestions. Three times a day, she went alone into a quiet room. She sat down comfortably in an armchair, relaxed her body, and closed her eyes. She stilled her mind and body as best she could. Physical inertia favors mental passivity and renders the mind more receptive to suggestion.

To counteract the fear suggestion, she repeated to herself, "I sing beautifully. I am poised, serene, confident, and calm." At each sitting she repeated this statement slowly, quietly, and with feeling from five to ten times. She had three such sittings during the day and one immediately before going to sleep.

After one week, she was completely poised and confident. When the fateful day came, she gave a wonderful audition and was cast in the part.

Develop a definite plan for turning over your requests or desires to your subconscious mind.

Never say, "I can't." Overcome that fear by substituting the following: "I can do all things through the power of my subconscious mind."

How She Restored Her Memory

A woman of seventy-five had always been proud of her ability to remember. Like everyone, she forgot things now and then, but she paid no attention. However, as she got older, she began to notice these occasions and worry about them. Each time she forgot something, she said to herself, "I must be losing my memory because of my age."

As a result of this negative autosuggestion, more and more names and events slipped her mind. She was close to despair. Then, fortunately, she realized how she was damaging herself. She resolved to reverse the process.

Every time she felt the temptation to think "I am losing my memory," she stopped herself. More than that, she deliberately reversed the procedure. Several times a day, she practiced induced positive autosuggestion. She said to herself:

From today onward, my memory is improving in every way. I will always remember whatever I need to know at every moment of time and point of space. The impressions I receive will be clear and definite. I will retain them automatically and easily. Whatever I want to recall will immediately present itself in the correct form in my mind. I am improving rapidly every day. Very soon my memory will be better than it has ever been before.

At the end of three weeks, her memory was back to normal.

How He Overcame a Nasty Temper

I was consulted by a man whose marriage and career were both in serious trouble. Hugh D.'s problem was his chronic irritability and bad temper. He was concerned about this himself, but if anyone tried to discuss it with him, he exploded in anger. He constantly told himself that everyone was picking on him and that he had to defend himself against them.

To counter this negative autosuggestion, I advised him to use positive autosuggestion. Several times a day—morning, noon, and at night prior to sleep—he was to repeat to himself:

From now on, I shall grow more good-humored. Joy, happiness, and cheerfulness are now becoming my normal states of mind. Every day I am becoming more and more lovable and understanding. I will be a center of cheer and goodwill to all those around me, infecting them with my good spirits. This happy, joyous, and cheerful mood is now becoming my normal, natural state of mind. I am grateful.

After a month, his wife and his coworkers remarked on how much easier he was to get along with.

Heterosuggestion

The term *heterosuggestion* means suggestions from another person. In all ages and in every part of the world, the power of suggestion has played a dominant part in the life and thought of humankind. Political creeds, religious beliefs, and cultural customs all flourish and perpetuate themselves through the power of heterosuggestion.

Suggestion can be used as a tool to discipline and control ourselves. However, it can also be used to take control and command over others who have not been taught to understand the laws of mind. In its constructive form it is wonderful and magnificent. In its negative aspects it is one of the most destructive of all the response patterns of the mind. Its results can be enduring patterns of misery, failure, suffering, sickness, and disaster.

Have You Accepted Any of These Negative Suggestions?

From the day we are born, we are bombarded with negative suggestions. Not knowing how to counter them, we unconsciously accept them and bring them into being as our experience.

Here are some examples of negative suggestions:

- You can't.

- You'll never amount to anything.

- You mustn't.

- You'll fail.

- You haven't got a chance.

- You're all wrong.

- It's no use.

- It's not what you know, but who you know.

- The world is going to the dogs.

- What's the use, nobody cares.

- There's no point to trying so hard.

- You're too old now.

- Things are getting worse and worse.

- Life is an endless grind.

- Love is for the birds.

- You just can't win.

- Watch out, you'll catch a terrible disease.

- You can't trust a soul.

By accepting heterosuggestions of this kind, you collaborate in bringing them to pass. As a child, you were helpless when faced with the suggestions of others who were important to you. You did not know any better. The mind, both conscious and unconscious, was a mystery you did not even wonder about.

As an adult, however, you are able to make choices. You can use constructive autosuggestion, which is a reconditioning therapy, to change the impressions made on you in the past. The first step is to make yourself aware of the heterosuggestions that are operating on you. Unexamined, they can create behavior patterns that cause failure in your personal and social life. Constructive autosuggestion can release you from the mass of negative verbal conditioning that might otherwise distort your life pattern, making the development of good habits difficult or even impossible.

You Can Counteract Negative Suggestions

Pick up the paper or turn on the television news. Every day, you hear dozens of stories that could sow the seeds of futility, fear, worry, anxiety, and impending doom. If you accept them and take them in, these thoughts of fear can cause you to lose the will for life. However, once you understand that you do not *have* to accept them, choices open up for you. You have within you the power to counteract all these destructive ideas by giving your subconscious mind constructive autosuggestions.

Check regularly on the negative suggestions that people make to you. You do not have to be at the mercy of destructive heterosuggestion. All of us have suffered from it in our childhood, in our teens, and in adulthood. If you look back, you can easily recall how parents, friends, relatives, teachers, and associates contributed in a campaign of negative suggestions. Study the things said to you, closely examine their underlying meaning, and you will discover that many of them were nothing more than a form of propaganda. Its concealed purpose was—and is—to control you by instilling fear in you.

This heterosuggestion process goes on in every home, office, factory, and club. You will find that many of the suggestions people make, whether they know it or not, are aimed at making you think, feel, and act as they want you to, in ways that are to their advantage, even if they are destructive to you.

How Suggestion Killed a Man

A distant relative of mine went to a celebrated crystal gazer in India and asked the woman to read his future. The seer told him that he had a bad heart. She predicted that he would die at the next new moon.

My relative was aghast. He called up everyone in his family and told them about the prediction. He met with his lawyer to make sure his will was up-to-date. When I tried to talk him out of his conviction, he told me that the crystal gazer was known to have amazing occult powers. She could do great good or harm to those she dealt with. He was convinced of the truth of this.

As the new moon approached, he became more and more withdrawn. A month before this man had been happy, healthy, vigorous, and robust. Now he was an invalid. On the date predicted, he suffered a fatal heart attack. He died not knowing he was the cause of his own death.

How many of us have heard similar stories and shivered a little at the thought that the world is full of mysterious uncontrollable forces? Yes, the world is full of forces, but they are neither mysterious nor uncontrollable. My relative killed himself, by allowing a powerful suggestion to enter into his subconscious mind. He believed in the crystal gazer's powers, so he accepted her prediction completely.

Let us take another look at what happened, knowing what we do about the way the subconscious mind works. *Whatever the conscious, reasoning mind of a person believes, the subconscious mind will accept and act upon.* My relative was in a suggestible state when he went to see the fortune-teller. She gave him a negative suggestion, and *he accepted it.* He became terrified. He constantly ruminated on his conviction that he was going to die at the next new moon. He told everyone about it, and he prepared for his end. It was his own fear and expectation of the end, accepted as true by his subconscious mind, that brought about his death.

The woman who predicted his death had no more power than the stones and sticks in the field. Her suggestion in itself had no power to create or bring about the end she suggested. If he had known the laws of his mind, he would have completely rejected the negative suggestion and refused to give her words any attention. He could have gone about the business of living with the secure knowledge that he was governed and controlled by his own thoughts and feelings. The prophecy of the seer would have been like a rubber ball thrown at an armored tank. He could have easily neutralized and dissipated her suggestion with no harm to himself. Instead, through lack of awareness and knowledge, he allowed it to kill him.

In themselves, the suggestions of others have no power over you. Whatever power they have, they gain because you give it to them through your own thoughts. You have to give your mental consent. You have to entertain and accept the thought. At that point it becomes your own thought, and your subconscious works to bring it into experience.

Remember you have the capacity to choose. Choose life! Choose love! Choose health!

The Promise of an Assumed Major Premise

Since the days of ancient Greece, philosophers and logicians have studied the form of reasoning called a *syllogism*. Your mind reasons in syllogisms. In practical terms, this means that whatever major premises your conscious mind assumes to be true, that determines the conclusion your subconscious mind will come to, no matter what the particular question or problem might be. If your premises are true, the conclusion *must* be true.

For example:

- All formed things change and pass away;

- the pyramids of Egypt are formed things;

- therefore, the pyramids will change and pass away.

And this:

- Every virtue is praiseworthy;

- kindness is a virtue;

- therefore, kindness is praiseworthy.

In both cases, the first statement is referred to as the major premise, and the right conclusion must necessarily follow the right premise.

A college professor who attended some of my science-of-mind lectures in New York City's Town Hall came to speak with me afterward. He told me, "Everything in my life is topsy-turvy. I have lost health, wealth, and friends. Everything I touch turns out wrong."

I explained to him that his problems followed logically and directly from his self-destructive major premise. To change his life, he had to establish a new major premise in his thinking. He needed to accept as true the conviction that the Infinite Intelligence of his subconscious mind was guiding, directing, and prospering him spiritually, mentally, and materially. Once he did that, his subconscious mind would automatically direct him wisely in his decisions, heal his body, and restore his mind to peace and tranquility.

This professor formulated an overall picture of the way he wanted his life to be. This was his major premise:

Infinite Intelligence leads and guides me in all my ways. Perfect health is mine, and the Law of Harmony operates in my mind and body. Beauty, love, peace, and abundance are mine. The principles of right action and divine order govern my entire life. I know my major premise is based on the eternal truths of life, and I know, feel, and believe that my subconscious mind responds according to the nature of my conscious mind's thinking.

Later he wrote me the following progress report: "I repeated the statements of my major premise slowly, quietly, and lovingly several times a day. I knew that they were sinking deep down into my subconscious mind. I was convinced by the laws of mind that results must follow. I am deeply grateful for the interview you gave me, and I would like to add that all departments of my life are changing for the better. It works!"

The Subconscious Does Not Argue Controversially

Your subconscious mind is all-wise. It knows the answers to all questions. However, it does not *know* that it knows. It does not argue with you or talk back to you. It does not say, "You must not impress me with suggestions of that sort."

When you say, "I can't do this," "I am too old now," "I can't meet this obligation," "I was born on the wrong side of the tracks," "I don't know the right politician," you are impregnating your subconscious with these negative thoughts. It responds accordingly. You are actually blocking your own good. You are bringing lack, limitation, and frustration into your life.

When you set up obstacles, impediments, and delays in your conscious mind, you are denying the wisdom and intelligence resident in your subconscious mind. You are actually saying in effect that your subconscious mind cannot solve your problem. This leads to mental and emotional congestion, followed by sickness and neurotic tendencies.

To realize your desires and overcome your frustration, affirm boldly several times a day:

The Infinite Intelligence that gave me this desire leads, guides, and reveals to me the perfect plan for the unfolding of my desire. I know the deeper wisdom of my subconscious is now responding, and what I feel and claim within is expressed in the without. There is a balance, equilibrium, and equanimity.

On the other hand, if you say, "There is no way out; I am lost; there is no way out of this dilemma; I am stymied and blocked," you will get no answer or response from your subconscious mind. If you want the subconscious to work for you, you have to give it the right request and get its cooperation. It is always working for you. It is controlling your heartbeat and breathing this minute. When you cut your finger, it sets in motion the complex process of healing. Its most fundamental tendency is lifeward. It is forever seeking to take care of you and preserve you.

Your subconscious has a mind of its own, but it accepts your patterns of thought and imagery. When you look for the answer to a problem, your subconscious will respond, but it expects you to come to a decision and to a true judgment in your conscious mind. You must acknowledge that the answer is in your subconscious mind. If you say, "I don't think there is any way out; I am all mixed up and confused; why don't I get an answer?" you are neutralizing your prayer. Like the soldier marking time, you use up vital energy but you do not move forward.

Still the wheels of your mind. Relax. Let go. Quietly affirm:

My subconscious knows the answer. It is responding to me now. I give thanks because I know the Infinite Intelligence of my subconscious knows all things and is revealing the perfect answer to me now. My real conviction is now setting free the majesty and glory of my subconscious mind. I rejoice that it is so.

IDEAS TO REMEMBER

1. Think good, and good follows. Think evil, and evil follows. You are what you think all day long.

2. Your subconscious mind does not argue with you. It accepts what your conscious mind decrees. If you say, "I can't afford it," your subconscious works to make it true. Select a better thought. Decree, "I'll buy it. I accept it in my mind."

3. You have the power to choose. Choose health and happiness. You can choose to be friendly, or you can choose to be unfriendly. Choose to be cooperative, joyous, friendly, lovable, and the whole world will respond. This is the best way to develop a wonderful personality.

4. Your conscious mind is the "watchman at the gate." Its chief function is to protect your subconscious mind from false impressions. Choose to believe that something good can happen and is happening now. Your greatest power is your capacity to choose. Choose happiness and abundance.

5. The suggestions and statements of others have no power to hurt you. The only power is the movement of your own thought. You can choose to reject the thoughts or statements of others and affirm the good. You have the power to choose how you will react.

6. Watch what you say. You have to account for every idle word. Never say, "I will fail; I will lose my job; I can't pay the rent." Your subconscious cannot take a joke. It brings all these things to pass.

7. Your mind is not evil. No force of nature is evil. It depends how you use the powers of nature. Use your mind to bless, heal, and inspire all people everywhere.

8. Never say, "I can't." Overcome that fear by substituting the following: "I can do all things through the power of my own subconscious mind."

9. Begin to think from the standpoint of the eternal truths and principles of life and not from the standpoint of fear, ignorance, and superstition. Do not let others do your thinking for you. Choose your own thoughts and make your own decisions.

10. You are the captain of your soul (subconscious mind) and the master of your fate. Remember, you have the capacity to choose. Choose life! Choose love! Choose health! Choose happiness!

11. Whatever your conscious mind assumes and believes to be true, your subconscious mind will accept and bring to pass. Believe in good fortune, divine guidance, right action, and all the blessings of life.

To picture the end result in your mind causes your subconscious to respond and fulfill your mental picture.

Chapter Three

The Miracle-Working Power of Your Subconscious Mind

It is foolish to believe in sickness and something to hurt or to harm you. Believe in perfect health, prosperity, peace, wealth, and divine guidance.

The power of your subconscious is beyond all measure. It inspires you and guides you. It calls up vivid scenes from the storehouse of memory. Your subconscious controls your heartbeat and the circulation of your blood. It regulates your digestion, assimilation, and elimination. When you eat a piece of bread, your subconscious mind transmutes it into tissue, muscle, bone, and blood. These processes are beyond the ken of the wisest person who walks the earth. Your subconscious mind controls all the vital processes and functions of your body. It knows the answer to all problems.

Your subconscious mind never sleeps, never rests. It is always on the job. You can discover the miracle-working power of your subconscious by plainly stating to your subconscious prior to sleep that you want a specific thing accomplished. You will be amazed and delighted to discover that forces within you will be released that lead to the result you wished for. Here is a source of power and wisdom that puts you directly in touch with omnipotence. This is the power that moves the world, guides the planets in their course, and causes the sun to shine.

Your subconscious mind is the source of your ideals, aspirations, and altruistic urges. It was through the subconscious mind that Shakespeare perceived and communicated great truths hidden from the average man of his day. It was through the subconscious mind that the Greek sculptor, Phidias, gained the art and skill to portray beauty, order, symmetry, and proportion in marble and bronze. The subconscious mind is the deep well from which great artists draw their awe-provoking power. It enabled the great Italian artist Raphael to paint his Madonnas, and the great German musician Beethoven to compose his symphonies.

While lecturing at the Yoga Forest University, in Rishikesh, India, I had a long conversation with a surgeon who was visiting from Bombay. From him, I learned the astonishing story of Dr. James Esdaille.

Esdaille was a Scottish surgeon who practiced in Bengal during the 1840s. This was before ether or other modern methods of chemical anesthesia were in use. Nevertheless, between 1843 and 1846, Dr. Esdaille performed some four hundred major surgical operations of all kinds. These included amputations, removal of tumors and cancerous growths, and operations on the eye, ear, and throat. All these operations were performed under mental anesthesia only. Patients said they felt no pain, and none of them died during surgery.

Just as amazing, the mortality rate of Esdaille's patients following surgery was extremely low. This was well before Western scientists such as Louis Pasteur and Joseph Lister pointed out the bacterial origin of infection. No one realized that post-operative infections were due to unsterilized instruments and virulent organisms. Nevertheless, when Esdaille suggested to his patients, who were in a hypnotic state, that no infection or septic condition would develop, their subconscious minds responded to his suggestion. They set in motion the processes needed to fight off the life-threatening dangers of infection.

Think of it: More than a century and a half ago, this Scottish surgeon who had gone halfway around the world discovered how to use the miraculous wonder-working powers of the subconscious mind. It is enough to cause you to be seized with awe. The transcendental powers that inspired Dr. Esdaille and that protected his patients from mortal danger can be yours, too.

Your subconscious mind can give you independence of time and space. It can make you free of all pain and suffering. It can give you the answer to all problems, whatever they may be. There is a power and an intelligence within you that far transcends your intellect, causing you to marvel at the wonder of it all. All these experiences cause you to rejoice and believe in the miracle-working powers of your own subconscious mind.

Your Subconscious Is Your Book of Life
Whatever thoughts, beliefs, opinions, theories, or dogmas you write, engrave, or impress on your subconscious mind, you will experience them as the objective manifestation of circumstances, conditions, and events. What you write on the inside, you will experience on the outside. You have two sides to your life, objective and subjective, visible and invisible, thought and its manifestation.

Your thought is received as a pattern of neural firings in your cerebral cortex, which is the organ of your conscious reasoning mind. Once your conscious or objective mind accepts the thought completely, it is transmitted to the older parts of the brain, where it becomes flesh and is made manifest in your experience.

As previously outlined, your subconscious cannot argue. It acts only from what you write on it. It accepts your verdict or the conclusions of your conscious mind as final. This is why you are always writing on the book of life, because your thoughts become your experiences. The American philosopher Ralph Waldo Emerson said, "Man is what he thinks all day long."

What Is *Impressed* in the Subconscious Is *Expressed*

William James, the father of American psychology, said that the power to move the world is in your subconscious mind. Your subconscious mind is one with Infinite Intelligence and Boundless Wisdom. It is fed by hidden springs and is called the law of life. Whatever you impress upon your subconscious mind, the latter will move heaven and earth to bring it to pass. You must, therefore, impress it with right ideas and constructive thoughts.

The reason there is so much chaos and misery in the world is that so many people do not understand the interaction of their conscious and subconscious minds. When these two principles are in accord, in concord, in peace, and synchronously together, you will have health, happiness, peace, and joy. There is no sickness or discord when the conscious and subconscious work together harmoniously and peacefully.

In the ancient world, Hermes Trismegistus had the reputation of being the greatest, most powerful magus the world had ever known. When his tomb was opened, centuries after his passing, those who were in touch with the wisdom of the ancients waited with great expectancy and a sense of wonder. It was said that the greatest secret of the ages would be found within the tomb. And so it was. The secret inscribed in the tomb read:

> *As within, so without;*
> *As above, so below.*

In other words, whatever you impress in your subconscious mind, that becomes expressed on the screen of space. This same truth was proclaimed by Moses, Isaiah, Jesus, Buddha, Zoroaster, Laotze, and all the illumined seers of the ages. Whatever you feel as true subjectively is expressed as conditions, experiences, and events. Motion and emotion must balance. As in heaven (your own mind), so on earth (in your body and environment). This is the great law of life.

You will find throughout all nature the law of action and reaction, of rest and motion. These two must balance and then there will be harmony and equilibrium. You are here to let the life-principle flow through you rhythmically and harmoniously. The intake and the outgo must be equal. The impression and the expression must be equal. All your frustration is due to unfulfilled desire.

If you think negatively, destructively, and viciously, these thoughts generate destructive emotions that must be expressed and must find an outlet. These negative emotions are frequently expressed as ulcers, heart trouble, tension, and anxieties.

What is your idea or feeling about yourself now? Every part of your being expresses that idea. Your vitality, body, financial condition, friends, and social status represent a perfect reflection of the idea you have of yourself. This is the real meaning of what is impressed in your subconscious mind and what is expressed in all phases of your life.

We injure ourselves by the negative ideas we entertain. How often have you wounded yourself by getting angry, fearful, jealous, or vengeful? These are the poisons that enter your subconscious mind. You were not born with these negative attitudes. Feed your subconscious mind life-giving thoughts and you will wipe out all the negative patterns lodged within it. As you continue to do this, all the past will be wiped out and remembered no more.

The Subconscious Heals a Malignancy of the Skin

The most convincing evidence anyone can have of the healing power of the subconscious mind is a personal healing. Many years ago I developed a malignancy of the skin. I went to the finest doctors, who tried the most advanced treatments medical science could offer. None of these helped. The malignancy got progressively worse.

Then, one day, a clergyman with a deep store of psychological knowledge told me the inner meaning of the 139th Psalm. He called my attention to the passage that reads:

> *Thou didst see my limbs unformed in the womb, and in thy book they are all recorded; day by day they were fashioned, not one of them was late in growing.* (Psalm 139:16)

He explained that the term "book" meant my subconscious mind, which fashioned and molded all my organs from a tiny original cell. He pointed out that since my subconscious mind had made my body, it could also recreate it and heal it according to the perfect pattern within it.

This clergyman pointed to his watch. "This had a maker," he told me. "But before the watch could become an objective reality, the watchmaker had to have the idea of it clearly in mind. If for some reason the watch stopped working as it should, the watchmaker's idea of it would give him the knowledge he needed to fix it."

I understood what he was trying to tell me by this analogy. The subconscious intelligence that created my body was like the watchmaker. It knew exactly how to heal, restore, and direct all the vital functions and processes of my body. But for it to do this properly, I had to give it the idea of perfect health. This would act as cause, and the effect would be a healing.

I formulated a very simple and direct prayer:

My body and all its organs were created by the Infinite Intelligence in my subconscious mind. It knows how to heal me. Its wisdom fashioned all my organs, tissues, muscles, and bones. This Infinite Healing Presence within me is now transforming every cell of my being, making me whole and perfect. I give thanks for the healing I know is taking place at this time. Wonderful are the works of the creative intelligence within me.

I repeated this simple prayer aloud for about five minutes two or three times a day. After some three months, my skin was whole and perfect. The malignancy had vanished. My doctor was baffled, but I knew what had happened. I had given life-giving patterns of wholeness, beauty, and perfection to my subconscious mind. These forced out the negative images and patterns of thought lodged in my subconscious mind, which were the cause of all my trouble.

Nothing appears on your body except when the mental equivalent is first in your mind. As you change your mind by drenching it with incessant affirmatives, you change your body. This is the basis of all healing.

> *All disease originates in the mind. Nothing appears on the body unless there is a mental pattern corresponding to it.*
>
> *There is one process of healing and that is faith. There is only one healing power, namely your subconscious mind.*
>
> *Find out what it is that heals you. Realize that correct directions given to your subconscious mind will heal your mind and body.*

How the Subconscious Controls All Functions of the Body

Whether you are awake or asleep, the ceaseless, tireless action of your subconscious mind controls all the vital functions of your body without any need for your conscious mind to intervene. While you are asleep, your heart continues to beat rhythmically. Your chest and diaphragm muscles pump air in and out of your lungs. There the carbon dioxide that is the by-product of the activity of your body's cells is exchanged for the fresh oxygen you need to go on functioning. Your subconscious controls your digestive processes and glandular secretions, as well as all the other wondrously complex operations of your body. All this happens whether you are awake or asleep.

If you were forced to operate your body's functions with your conscious mind, you would certainly fail; you would probably die a very quick death. The processes are too complicated, too intertwined. The "heart-lung" machine that is used during open-heart surgery is one of the wonders of modern medical technology, but what it does is infinitely simpler than what your subconscious mind does twenty-four hours a day, year in, year out.

Suppose you were crossing the ocean in a supersonic jetliner and you wandered into the cockpit. You certainly would not know how to fly the plane, but you would not find it difficult to distract the pilot and cause a problem. In the same way, your conscious mind cannot operate your body, but it can get in the way of proper operation.

Worry, anxiety, fear, and depression interfere with the normal functioning of the heart, lungs, stomach, and intestines. The medical community is just beginning to appreciate the seriousness of so-called stress-related diseases. The reason is that these patterns of thought interfere with the harmonious functioning of your subconscious mind.

When you feel physically and mentally disturbed, the best thing you can do is to let go, relax, and still the wheels of your thought processes. Speak to your subconscious mind. Tell it to take over in peace, harmony, and divine order. You will find that all the functions of your body will become normal again. Be sure to speak to your subconscious mind with authority and conviction. It will respond by carrying out your command.

How to Get the Subconscious to Work for You

The first thing to realize is that your subconscious mind is always working. It is active night and day, whether you act upon it or not. Your subconscious is the builder of your body, but you cannot consciously perceive or hear that inner silent process. Your business is with your conscious mind and not your subconscious mind. Just keep your conscious mind busy with the expectation of the best, and make sure the thoughts you habitually think are based on things that are lovely, true, just, and harmonious. Begin now to take care of your conscious mind, knowing in your heart and soul that your subconscious mind is always expressing, reproducing, and manifesting according to your habitual thinking.

Remember, just as water takes the shape of the pipe it flows through, the life-principle in you flows through you according to the nature of your thoughts. Claim that the healing presence in your subconscious is flowing through you as harmony, health, peace, joy, and abundance. Think of it as a living intelligence, a lovely companion on the way. Firmly believe it is continually flowing through you vivifying, inspiring, and prospering you. It will respond exactly this way. It is done unto you as you believe.

Ruling Principle of the Subconscious Restores Optic Nerves

One of the most celebrated healing shrines in the world is at Lourdes, in southwestern France. The archives of the medical department of Lourdes are filled with dossiers that detail well-authenticated cases of what are termed miraculous healings. One example among many is the case of Madame Bire, who was blind, with optic nerves that were atrophied and useless. After she visited Lourdes, she regained her sight. Several doctors who examined her testified that her optic nerves were still useless, and yet, she saw! A month later, a reexamination found that her visual mechanism had been fully restored to normal.

I am thoroughly convinced that Madame Bire was *not* healed by the waters of the shrine. What healed her was her own subconscious mind, which responded to her belief. The healing principle within her subconscious mind responded to the nature of her thought. Belief is a thought in the subconscious mind. It means to accept something as true. The thought accepted executes itself automatically.

Undoubtedly, Madame Bire went to the shrine with expectancy and great faith. She knew in her heart she would receive a healing. Her subconscious mind responded accordingly, releasing the ever-present healing forces. The subconscious mind that created the eye can certainly bring a dead nerve back to life. What the creative principle created, it can recreate. *According to your faith is it done unto you.*

How to Convey the Idea of Perfect Health to Your Subconscious

A Methodist minister I met in Johannesburg, South Africa, told me how he overcame an advanced case of lung cancer. The method he used was to convey the idea of perfect health to his subconscious mind. At my request, he sent me a detailed description of the process, which I now pass along to you.

Several times a day I would make certain that I was completely relaxed mentally and physically. I relaxed my body by speaking to it as follows:

"My feet are relaxed, my ankles are relaxed, my legs are relaxed, my abdominal muscles are relaxed, my heart and lungs are relaxed, my head is relaxed, my whole being is completely relaxed."

After about five minutes I would find myself drifting into a sleepy, drowsy state. Then I affirmed the following truth:

"The perfection of God is now being expressed through me. The idea of perfect health is now filling my subconscious mind. The image God has of me is a perfect image, and my subconscious mind recreates my body in perfect accordance with the perfect image held in the mind of God."

This minister had a remarkable healing. The technique he used is a simple, straightforward way of conveying the idea of perfect health to your subconscious mind.

Another wonderful way to convey the idea of health to your subconscious is through disciplined or scientific imagination. I told a man who was suffering from functional paralysis to make a vivid picture of himself walking around in his office, touching the desk, answering the telephone, and doing all the things he ordinarily would do if he were healed. I explained to him that this mental visualization of perfect health would be accepted by his subconscious mind.

He threw himself into the role. He actually felt himself back in the office. He knew that he was giving his subconscious mind something concrete and definite to work upon. His subconscious mind was the film upon which the visualization was impressed.

He continued this visualization discipline intensively for several weeks. Then, one day, the telephone rang at a time when everyone else was out. The telephone was twelve feet away from his bed. Nevertheless, he managed to answer it. His paralysis vanished from that hour on. The healing power of his subconscious mind had responded to his mental imagery, and a healing followed.

This man had suffered from a mental block that prevented nerve impulses generated in the brain from reaching his legs. Therefore, he could not walk. When he shifted his attention to the healing power within him, the power flowed through his focused attention, and he could walk again.

Whatever you pray for in faith, you will receive.
(Matthew 21:22)

IDEAS TO REMEMBER

1. Your subconscious mind controls all the vital processes of your body and knows the answer to all problems.

2. Prior to sleep, turn over a specific request to your subconscious mind and prove its miracle-working power to yourself.

3. Whatever you impress on your subconscious mind is expressed on the screen of space as conditions, experiences, and events. Therefore, you should carefully watch all ideas and thoughts entertained in your conscious mind.

4. The law of action and reaction is universal. Your thought is action, and the reaction is the automatic response of your subconscious mind to your thought. Watch your thoughts!

5. All frustration is due to unfulfilled desires. If you dwell on obstacles, delays, and difficulties, your subconscious mind responds accordingly, and you are blocking your own good.

6. The life-principle will flow through. Feed your subconscious with thoughts of harmony, health, and peace, and all the functions of your body will become normal again.

7. Keep your conscious mind busy with the expectation of the best, and your subconscious will faithfully reproduce your habitual thinking.

8. Imagine the happy ending or solution to your problem,

feel the thrill of accomplishment, and what you imagine and feel will be accepted by your subconscious mind, which will bring it to pass.

9. You must consciously affirm: "I believe that the subconscious power that gave me this desire is now fulfilling it through me." This dissolves all conflicts.

Imagine the end desired and feel its reality. Follow it through and you will get definite results.

Chapter Four

Mental Healings in Ancient Times

Think good and good follows. Think evil and evil follows. You are what you think all day long.

Through the ages, people in every continent, climate, and culture have instinctively known that somewhere there resided a healing power that could restore the abilities and functions of a person's body to its normal state of efficiency and good health. They believed that this strange power could be invoked under certain conditions and that if it were invoked properly, the alleviation of human suffering would follow. The history of all nations presents testimony in support of this belief.

In the early history of the world, the power of secretly influencing people for good or evil, including the healing of the sick, was said to be possessed by priests, priestesses, and holy people. They claimed to possess powers derived directly from God that included the healing of the sick. The procedures and processes of healing varied throughout the world, but they generally included supplications and offerings to the god; various ceremonies, such as the laying on of hands and incantations; and the use of amulets, talismans, rings, relics, and images.

For example, in the religions of antiquity priests in the ancient temples gave drugs to their patients and practiced hypnotic suggestions as they went to sleep. The patients were told that the gods would surely visit them in their sleep and heal them. Many healings followed.

The devotees of Hecate were told to mix lizards with resin, frankincense, and myrrh and pound all this together in the open air under the crescent moon. After performing these bizarre and mysterious rites, they prayed to the goddess, took the potion they had just compounded, and went to sleep. If their faith was strong enough, they saw the goddess in a dream. This rite, which sounds so strange, even fantastic, to our ears, was often followed by healings.

People in ancient times worked out many effective ways to tap the incredible power of the subconscious mind and use it for healing. While they knew that these procedures worked, however, they did not understand how or why they worked. Today, we can see that they were using potent suggestions to the subconscious mind. The rituals and potions and amulets appealed powerfully to the imagination of people and favored the acceptance by the subconscious mind of the insistent suggestions given by the healer. But the *work* of healing was done by the patient's own subconscious mind.

In all ages unofficial healers have obtained remarkable results in cases where authorized medical skill had failed and the patients had given up hope. This gives cause for thought. How do these healers in all parts of the world effect their cures? The answer is that these healings take place because the belief of the sick person released the healing power resident in his or her subconscious mind. The more fantastic and peculiar the remedies and methods used by the healers, the more likely the patients were to believe that anything so strange must be unusually powerful. Their aroused emotional state made it easier for them to accept the suggestion of health, in both their conscious and subconscious mind.

Biblical Accounts on the Use of the Subconscious Powers

What things soever ye desire, when ye pray, believe that ye receive them, and ye shall have them. (Mark 11:24; King James)

Reread this passage from the apostle Mark and pay close attention to the difference in tenses. The verbs *believe* and *receive* are in the present, but the phrase *shall have* is in the future. The inspired writer is telling us something of the greatest importance by this seemingly minor difference in the grammar of the sentence. If we believe and accept as true the fact that our desire has *already* been accomplished and fulfilled, that it is *already* completed, then its realization will follow as a thing in *the future.*

The success of this technique relies on the confident conviction that the thought, the idea, the picture is already fact in mind. In order for anything to have substance in the realm of mind, it must be thought of as actually existing.

Here in a few words is a concise and specific direction for making use of the creative power of thought by impressing upon the subconscious the particular thing you desire. Your thought, idea, plan, or purpose is as real on its own plane as your hand or your heart. In following the biblical technique, you completely eliminate from your mind all consideration of conditions, circumstances, or anything that might imply a negative outcome. You are planting a seed (concept) in the mind that, if you leave it undisturbed, will infallibly germinate into external fruition.

The prime condition that Jesus insisted upon was faith.

Over and over again you read in the Bible, "According to your *faith* is it done unto you." If you plant certain types of seeds in the ground, you have faith they will grow after their kind. This is the way of seeds, and trusting the laws of growth and agriculture, you know that the seeds will come forth after their kind.

The faith that is described in the Bible is a way of thinking, an attitude of mind, an inner certitude, knowing that the idea you fully accept in your conscious mind will be embodied in your subconscious mind and made manifest. Faith is, in a sense, accepting as true what your reason and senses deny. It is closing down, refusing to listen to the little, rational, analytical, conscious mind and embracing an attitude of complete reliance on the inner power of your subconscious mind.

Here is one of the best-known examples of the biblical technique of healing:

And when he had gone indoors they [two blind men] came to him. Jesus asked, "Do you believe that I have the power to do what you want?" "Yes sir," they said. Then he touched their eyes, and said, "As you have believed, so let it be"; and their sight was restored. Jesus said to them sternly, "See that no one hears about this." (Matthew 9:28–30)

By saying "according to your faith it is done unto you," Jesus was openly appealing to the cooperation of the subconscious mind of the blind men. Their faith was their great expectancy, their inner feeling, their inner conviction that something miraculous would happen, that their prayer would be answered. And therefore it was. This is the time-honored technique of healing, utilized alike by all healing groups throughout the world, regardless of religious affiliation.

In saying, "see that no one hears about this," Jesus was urging the healed patients not to discuss their healing with others. If they did so, they might be harassed by the skeptical and derogatory criticisms of the unbelieving. This in turn might have tended to undo the benefits they had received at the hand of Jesus by depositing thoughts of fear, doubt, and anxiety in the subconscious mind.

When the sick came to Jesus to be healed, they were healed by their own faith, together with his faith and understanding of the healing power of the subconscious mind. Whatever he decreed, he felt inwardly to be true. He and the people needing help were in the one universal subjective mind, and his silent inner knowing and conviction of the healing power changed the negative destructive patterns in the patients' subconscious. The resultant healings were the automatic response to the internal mental change. His command was his appeal to the subconscious mind of the patients plus his awareness, feeling, and absolute trust in the response of the subconscious mind to the words that he spoke with authority.

Miracles at Various Shrines Throughout the World

On every continent, in every land, there are shrines at which cures take place. Some are world famous, like Lourdes, and others are known only to those who live nearby. Whether celebrated or obscure, the healings that take place at these shrines happen for the same reasons and by way of the same powers of the subconscious mind.

I have visited several of the famous shrines in Japan. The central focus of the world-renowned shrine of Daibutsu is a gigantic bronze statue, forty-two feet tall. It depicts Buddha seated with folded hands, his head inclined in an attitude of profound contemplative ecstasy.

Here I saw young and old making offerings at its feet. Money, fruit, rice, and oranges were offered. Candles were lit, incense was burned, and prayers of petition were recited. I listened to the chant of a young girl as she intoned a prayer, bowed low, and placed two oranges as an offering. She was thanking Buddha for restoring her voice. She had lost her voice, but it was restored at the shrine. Her simple faith that Buddha would give her back her singing voice if she followed a certain ritual, fasted, and made certain offerings had helped to kindle faith and expectancy. The result was a conditioning of her mind to the point of belief. Her subconscious mind then responded to her belief.

The power of imagination and blind belief cannot be overstated. A wondrous example of this is the case of a relative of mine in Perth, in western Australia, who suffered from tuberculosis. His lungs were badly diseased. His son decided to help his father heal himself. He went to his father's home and told him he had recently met a wandering monk with strange powers.

This monk had just returned from a long stay at one of the most celebrated healing shrines in Europe. There he had acquired a small fragment of the True Cross, set in a ring dating back from the Middle Ages. Over the centuries, countless sufferers had been healed after touching the ring or the fragment of the Cross.

When the son had heard this he had told the monk about his father's illness and begged to borrow the ring. The monk had agreed. The son then gave the monk a free-will offering of the equivalent of $500.

When the son showed his father the ring, the older man practically snatched it from him. He clasped the ring to his chest, prayed silently, and went to sleep. In the morning he was healed. All the clinic's tests proved negative.

Healings of this sort happen all the time. What is most significant about this one is that the son's amazing story was totally made up. In fact, he had picked up a splinter of ordinary wood from the sidewalk, taken it to a jeweler, and had it set in a gold ring of antique design. He then gave it to his father.

You know, of course, it was not the splinter of wood from the sidewalk that healed the father. No, it was his imagination aroused to an intense degree, plus the confident expectancy of a perfect healing. Imagination was joined to faith or subjective feeling, and the union of the two brought about a healing through the power of his subconscious mind.

The father never learned of the trick that had been played upon him. If he had, he might well have had a relapse. Instead, his tuberculosis never returned. He remained completely cured and passed away from other causes fifteen years later, at the age of eighty-nine.

Know that faith is like a seed planted in the ground; it grows after its kind. Plant the idea (seed) in your mind, water and fertilize it with expectancy and it will manifest.

Be a mental engineer and use tried and proved techniques in building a grander and greater life.

Learn to pray for your loved ones who may be ill. Quiet your mind and your thoughts of healing, vitality, and perfection operating through the one universal subjective mind will be felt and resurrected in the mind of your loved one.

One Universal Healing Principle

It is a well-known fact that all the various schools of healing bring about documented cures of the most wonderful character. The most obvious conclusion that strikes your mind is that there must be some underlying organ and process that is common to them all. Indeed there is. The organ of healing is the subconscious mind, and the process of healing is faith.

Think deeply about these fundamental truths:

- You possess mental functions that have been distinguished by designating one the conscious mind and the other the subconscious mind.

- Your subconscious mind is constantly amenable to the power of suggestion.

- Your subconscious mind has complete control of the functions, conditions, and sensations of your body.

You surely know that symptoms of almost any disease can be induced in hypnotic subjects by suggestion. For example, a subject in the hypnotic state can develop a high temperature, flushed face, or chills according to the nature of the suggestion given. You can suggest to the person that he is paralyzed and cannot walk, and it will be so. You can hold a cup of cold water under the nose of the hypnotic subject and tell him, "This is full of pepper; smell it!" He will sneeze violently and repeatedly. What do you think caused him to sneeze? The water, or the suggestion?

If someone tells you he is allergic to timothy grass, you can place a synthetic flower or an empty glass in front of his nose, when he is in a hypnotic state, and tell him it is timothy grass.

He will develop his usual allergic symptoms. This shows us that the cause of the symptoms is in the subconscious mind. Curing the symptoms also takes place in the subconscious mind.

Different schools of medicine, such as osteopathy, chiropractic, chi-gong, acupuncture, and naturopathy, all produce remarkable healings. So do the rites and ceremonies of the various religious beliefs throughout the world. It is obvious that all of these healings are brought about through the subconscious mind—the only healer there is.

Notice how the subconscious mind heals a cut on your finger. It knows exactly how to do it. The doctor dresses the wound and says, "Nature heals it!" But "nature" is nothing more than another name for natural law, the law of the subconscious mind. The instinct of self-preservation is the first law of nature, and self-preservation is the foremost function of the subconscious mind. Your strongest instinct is the most potent of all autosuggestions.

Widely Differing Theories of Healing

Many different theories of healing have been advanced by different religious sects and prayer-therapy groups. There are a great number who claim that because their practice produces results, their theory therefore must be right. As we have seen in this chapter, this cannot be correct.

As you know, there are many varieties of healing. Franz Anton Mesmer (1734–1815), an Austrian physician who practiced in Paris, discovered that by applying magnets to a diseased body, he could cure that disease miraculously. He also performed cures with various other pieces of glass and metal. Later, he abandoned the use of these objects in favor of passing his hands over the patient's body. He claimed that the real source of his cures was what he called "animal magnetism." He theorized that some mysterious magnetic substance was transmitted from the healer's hands to the patient.

Mesmer lent his name to this method of treating disease, which came to be called mesmerism. Today we know it as hypnotism. Other physicians, jealous of Mesmer's success, claimed that all his healings were due to suggestion and nothing else. When pressed, however, they had to admit that they did not know how this power of suggestion created such amazing effects.

All of these groups—psychiatrists, psychologists, osteopaths, chiropractors, physicians, and religious groups of every variety—are using the one universal power resident in the subconscious mind. Each may proclaim the healings are due to their theory, but the truth is far different. The process of all healing is a definite, positive, mental attitude, an inner attitude, or a way of thinking, called faith. Healing is due to a confident expectancy that acts as a powerful suggestion to the subconscious mind, releasing its healing potency.

One person does not heal by a different power than another. It is true that both may have their own theories or methods, but there is only one process of healing, and that is faith. There is only one healing power; namely, your subconscious mind. Select whatever theory, belief, and method that calls out to you. You can rest assured, if you have faith, you will get results.

View of Paracelsus

Philippus Paracelsus, a famous Swiss alchemist and physician, who lived from 1493 to 1541, was a great healer in his day. He stated what is now an obvious scientific fact when he said:

Whether the object of your faith be real or false, you will nevertheless obtain the same effects. Thus, if I believed in

Saint Peter's statue as I should have believed in Saint Peter himself, I shall obtain the same effects that I should have obtained from Saint Peter. But that is superstition. Faith, however, produces miracles; and whether it is true or false faith, it will always produce the same wonders.

The views of Paracelsus were echoed in the sixteenth century by Pietro Pomponazzi, an Italian philosopher, who wrote:

We can easily conceive the marvelous effects which confidence and imagination can produce, particularly when both qualities are reciprocated between the subjects and the person who influences them. The cures attributed to the influence of certain relics are the effect of their imagination and confidence. Quacks and philosophers know that if the bones of any skeleton were put in place of the saint's bones, the sick would nonetheless experience beneficial effects, if they believed that they were veritable relics.

Think what this implies. If you believe in the power of saints' bones, or in the healing properties of certain waters, or, like my Australian relative, in the miraculous effects of a fragment of wood, *you will get results* because of the powerful suggestion given to your subconscious mind. It is the latter that does the healing.

Bernheim's Experiments
Hippolyte Bernheim was professor of medicine at Nancy, France, early in the twentieth century. He was one of the first to explain how a physician's suggestion to the patient took effect because of the force of the subconscious mind.

Bernheim relates the story of a man whose tongue was paralyzed. Every form of treatment was tried, with no success at all.

Then one day the man's doctor announced that he had learned of a new instrument that was certain to relieve his problem. The doctor then put a pocket thermometer in the patient's mouth. The patient imagined this was the instrument that was to save him. In a few moments he cried out joyfully that he could once more move his tongue freely.

Bernheim continues:

> Among our cases, facts of the same sort will be found. A young girl came into my office, having suffered from complete loss of speech for nearly four weeks. After making sure of the diagnosis, I told my students that loss of speech sometimes yielded instantly to electricity, which might act simply by its suggestive influence. I sent for the induction apparatus. I applied my hand over the larynx and moved a little and said, "Now you can speak aloud." In an instant I made her say "a," then "b," then "Maria." She continued to speak distinctly; the loss of voice had disappeared.

Here Bernheim is showing the power of faith and expectancy on the part of the patient, which acts as a powerful suggestion to the subconscious mind.

Producing a Blister by Suggestion

Bernheim states that he produced a blister on the back of a patient's neck by applying a postage stamp and suggesting to the patient that it was a bee sting. This sort of demonstration has been confirmed by the experiments and experiences of many doctors in many parts of the world. These leave no doubt that structural changes in the body can be brought about as a result of oral suggestion to patients.

The Cause of Bloody Stigmata

Hemorrhages and bloody stigmata can be induced by means of suggestion.

As a demonstration of this, Dr. H. Bernheim put a subject into a hypnotic trance, then gave him the following suggestion:

> At four o'clock this afternoon, after the hypnosis, you will come into my office, sit down in this armchair and fold your arms across your chest. Your nose will then begin to bleed.

That afternoon, the young man did exactly as he had been told. After he crossed his arms, several drops of blood came from his left nostril.

On another occasion, the same investigator traced a patient's name on both his forearms with the dull point of an instrument while the patient was in a hypnotic trance. Bernheim then said:

> At four o'clock this afternoon you will go to sleep. Your arms will bleed along the lines I have traced, and your name will appear written on your arms in letters of blood.

The patient was carefully observed that afternoon. At four o'clock he fell asleep. On his left arm the letters stood out in bright relief, and in several places there were drops of blood. Although the letters gradually faded, they were still faintly visible three months afterward.

These facts demonstrate at once the correctness of the two fundamental propositions previously stated; namely, the constant amenability of the subconscious mind to the power of suggestion and the perfect control that the subconscious mind exercises over the functions, sensations, and conditions of the body.

All the foregoing phenomena dramatize vividly abnormal conditions induced by suggestion. They are conclusive proof that *as a man thinketh in his heart* [subconscious mind] *so is he*.

IDEAS TO REMEMBER

1. Remind yourself frequently that the healing power is in your subconscious mind.

2. Know that faith is like a seed planted in the ground; it grows after its kind. Plant the idea (seed) in your mind, water and fertilize it with expectancy, and it will become manifest.

3. The idea you have for a book, new invention, or play is real in your mind. This is why you can believe you have it now. Believe in the reality of your idea, plan, or invention, and as you do, it will become manifest.

4. In praying for another, know that your silent inner knowing of wholeness, beauty, and perfection can change the negative patterns of the other's subconscious mind and bring about wonderful results.

5. The miraculous healings you hear about at various shrines are due to imagination and blind faith that act on the subconscious mind, releasing the healing power.

6. All disease originates in the mind. Nothing appears on the body unless there is a mental pattern corresponding to it.

7. The symptoms of almost any disease can be induced in you by hypnotic suggestion. This shows you the power of your thought.

8. There is only one process of healing and that is faith. There is only one healing power; namely, your subconscious mind.

9. Whether the object of your faith is real or false, you will get results. Your subconscious mind responds to the thought in your mind. Look upon faith as a thought in your mind, and that will suffice.

The feeling of health produces health; the feeling of wealth produces wealth. How do you feel?

Chapter Five

Mental Healings
in Modern Times

*Think and plan independently of traditional methods. Know that
there is always an answer and a solution to every problem.*

What is it that heals? Where is this healing power, and how can
it be put to practical use? These are vital questions of deep con-
cern to all of us. To all of them, the answer is the same: This
healing power is in the subconscious mind of every person, and
a changed mental attitude on the part of the sick person releases
this healing power.

No mental- or religious-science practitioner, psychologist,
psychiatrist, or medical doctor ever healed a patient. There is an
old saying, "The doctor dresses the wound, but God heals it."
The psychologist or psychiatrist makes effective change by re-
moving the mental blocks in the patient so that the healing
principle may be released, restoring the patient to health. In the
same way, the surgeon removes the physical block, enabling the
healing currents to function normally. No physician, surgeon,

or mental-science practitioner can legitimately claim that he or she "healed the patient." The one healing power may be called by many different names—nature, life, God, creative intelligence—but in reality these are simply different ways to refer to subconscious power.

As we have already seen, there are many different ways we can use to remove the mental, emotional, and physical blocks that inhibit the flow of the healing life-principle animating all of us. The healing principle resident in your subconscious mind can and will, if properly directed by you or some other person, heal your mind and body of all disease. This healing principle operates in all people regardless of creed, color, or race. You do not have to belong to some particular church in order to use and participate in this healing process. Your subconscious will heal the burn or cut on your hand even if you profess to be an atheist or agnostic.

Modern mental healing is based on the truth that the Infinite Intelligence and power of your subconscious mind responds according to your faith. Mental-science practitioners or ministers follow the injunction of the Bible. That is, they go into their closet and shut the door, which means they still their minds, relax, let go, and think of the Infinite Healing Presence within them. They close the door of their mind to all outside distractions as well as appearances, and then they quietly and knowingly turn over their request or desire to their subconscious mind, realizing that the intelligence of their mind will answer them according to their specific needs.

The most wonderful thing to know is this: Imagine the end desired and feel its reality; then the infinite life-principle will respond to your conscious choice and your conscious request. This is the meaning of the text *believe you have received, and you shall receive.* This is what the modern mental scientist does when he or she practices prayer therapy.

One Process of Healing

There is only one universal healing principle operating through everything. We can consciously direct it to bless ourselves in countless ways.

There are many different approaches, techniques, and methods in using the universal power, but there is only one process of healing, which is faith, for *according to your faith is it done unto you.*

The Law of Belief

All religions of the world represent forms of belief, and these beliefs are explained in many ways. The law of life is belief. What do you believe about yourself, life, and the universe? *Whatever you pray for in faith, you shall receive.*

Belief is a thought in your mind that causes the power of your subconscious to be distributed into all phases of your life according to your thinking habits. You must realize that when the Bible speaks of belief, it is not talking about your belief in some ritual, ceremony, form, institution, or formula. It is talking about belief itself. The belief of your mind is simply the thought of your mind.

Everything is possible to one who has faith. (Mark 9:23)

It is foolish to believe in something that will hurt or harm you. Remember, it is not the thing believed in that hurts or harms you, but the belief or thought in your mind that creates the result. All your experiences, all your actions, and all the events and circumstances of your life are but the reflections and reactions to your own thought.

The Conscious and Subconscious Minds Scientifically Directed

Prayer or meditation therapy is the synchronized, harmonious, and intelligent function of the conscious and subconscious levels of mind specifically directed for a definite purpose. In scientific prayer or prayer therapy, you must know what you are doing and why you are doing it. You trust the law of healing. Prayer or meditation therapy is sometimes referred to as mental or psychological treatment. Another term is *scientific prayer.*

In this form of therapy you consciously choose a certain idea, mental picture, or plan that you desire to experience. You realize your capacity to convey this idea or mental image to your subconscious by feeling the reality of the state assumed. As you remain faithful in your mental attitude, your prayer or meditation will be answered. Such therapy is a definite mental action for a definite specific purpose.

Let us suppose that you decide to heal a certain difficulty by prayer or meditation therapy. You are aware that your problem or sickness, whatever it may be, must be caused by negative thoughts charged with fear and lodged in your subconscious mind. You realize that if you can succeed in cleansing your mind of these thoughts, you will get a healing.

You, therefore, turn to the healing power within your subconscious mind. You remind yourself of its Infinite Power and Intelligence and its capacity to heal all conditions. As you dwell on these truths, your fear will begin to dissolve. The recollection of these truths battles and ultimately overcomes the erroneous beliefs.

You give thanks for the healing that you know will come. Then you keep your mind off the difficulty until you feel guided, after an interval, to pray or meditate again. While you are so doing, you refuse to give any power to the negative conditions or to admit for a second that the healing will not come. This attitude of mind brings about the harmonious union of the conscious and subconscious mind, which releases the healing power.

Faith Healing: What It Means and How Blind Faith Works

What is popularly known as faith healing is *not* the faith spoken of in the Bible, which means knowledge of the interaction of the conscious and subconscious mind. A faith healer is one who heals without any real scientific understanding of the powers and forces involved. He or she may claim a special gift of healing, and the sick person's blind belief in him or her or in his or her powers may bring results.

In many parts of the world, traditional healers treat their patients by dances, incantations, and invocations of spirits. A person may be healed by touching the relics of a saint, wearing special ritual garb, lighting a holy incense stick or a candle, or drinking a mixture of brewed herbs. *Anything* that leads the patient to honestly believe in the method or process will make a healing more likely.

Any method that causes you to move from fear and worry to faith and expectancy will heal. Many people claim that because their individual theories produce results, they must therefore be correct and true. As we have already seen, this cannot be right.

To illustrate how blind faith works, think back to our discussion of the Swiss physician, Franz Anton Mesmer. In 1776 he claimed to have produced many cures by stroking the bodies of his patients with magnets. As noted in the previous chapter, he changed his method and threw away his magnets and simply made passes with his hands at a short distance from the patient. This, too, worked. To explain the success of this new procedure, Mesmer evolved the theory, which he called *animal magnetism*. This he claimed was a fluid that pervades the universe but is most active in the human organism. He claimed that this magnetic fluid was being transmitted from his hands to the diseased bodies of his patients and that this transfer of animal magnetism was what healed them. People flocked to him, and many wonderful cures were reported.

Mesmer moved to Paris. There the government appointed a commission to investigate his cures. Its members included prominent physicians and members of the Academy of Science, of which Benjamin Franklin was a member. After a thorough inquiry, the commission admitted that Mesmer had produced confirmed cures. It held, however, that there was no evidence to prove the correctness of his magnetic-fluid theory. It suggested that the effects were due to the imagination of the patients.

Soon after this, Mesmer was driven into exile. He died in 1815. Shortly afterward, Dr. James Braid of Manchester, England, undertook to show that magnetic fluid had nothing to do with the production of the healings of Dr. Mesmer. Dr. Braid discovered that patients could be thrown into hypnotic sleep by suggestion. While they were in the hypnotic trance, he succeeded in producing many of the amazing phenomena that Mesmer had ascribed to animal magnetism.

You can readily see that all these cures were undoubtedly brought about by the active imagination of the patients together with a powerful suggestion of health to their subconscious minds. It is not unfair to call this blind faith, because neither the patients nor the practitioners understood how the cures were brought about.

Your mind is not evil. No force of nature is evil. It depends upon how you use the powers of nature. Use your mind to bless, heal, and inspire all people everywhere.

You build a new body every eleven months. Change your body by changing your thoughts and keeping them changed.

When your mind is relaxed and you accept an idea, your subconscious goes to work to accept the idea.

Subjective Faith

The subjective or subconscious mind of an individual is as amenable to the control of his or her own conscious or objective mind as it is to the suggestions of another. It follows that whatever may be your objective belief, if you will assume to have faith actively or passively, your subconscious mind will be controlled by the suggestion, and your desire will be fulfilled.

The faith required in mental healings is a purely subjective faith. The way to attain it is to put an end to active opposition on the part of the objective or conscious mind. For an effective healing of the body to take place, it is, of course, best if both the conscious and subconscious mind are in a state of fully accepting faith. However, it is not always essential. You can enter into a condition of passivity and receptivity by relaxing the mind and the body and getting into a sleepy state. In this drowsy state your passivity becomes receptive to subjective impression.

A man once asked me, "How is it that I got a healing through a certain minister? When he told me that there is no such thing as disease and that matter does not exist, I did not believe a word he said. I thought he was insulting my intelligence. And yet, I was healed. How could that be?"

As I told this man, the explanation is simple. He was quieted by soothing words and told to get into a perfectly passive condition, to say nothing and think of nothing for the time being. The minister also became passive. He affirmed quietly, peacefully, and constantly for about a half hour that this man would have perfect health, peace, harmony, and wholeness.

At the end of the half hour, the man felt immense relief and was restored to health.

It is easy to see that his subjective faith had been made manifest by his passivity under treatment, and the suggestions of perfect healthfulness by the minister were conveyed to his subconscious mind. The two subjective minds were then in rapport.

If the man had allowed his doubts about the healer's power and the correctness of his theory to surface, these would have acted as antagonistic autosuggestions. The minister's suggestions would have been seriously handicapped or even totally frustrated. In this sleepy, drowsy state, however, the resistance of the conscious mind was reduced to a minimum. The subconscious mind of the patient was receptive to the minister's suggestions. It performed its functions in harmony with those suggestions, and a healing followed.

The Meaning of Absent Treatment

Suppose while living in Los Angeles, you learned that your mother in New York City was seriously ill. Your first impulse might be to leave your home and job to go to her. But what if that were not possible? Would you have to give up any hope of lending the strength of your faith to the process of your mother's recovery?

No. While you might not be physically present, your prayers would go to her nonetheless. It is the Father within that doeth the work.

There is but one creative mind. The creative law of mind serves you. What you must do is induce an inner realization of health and harmony in your own mentality. Its response is automatic. This inner realization, acting through the subconscious mind, operates in turn on your mother's subconscious mind. Your thoughts of health, vitality, and perfection operate through the one universal subjective mind. They set in motion a law of the subjective side of life that manifests itself through her body as a healing.

In the mind principle, there is no time or space. The same mind operates through your mother—and through you—no matter where you may be. In reality there is no absent treatment as opposed to present treatment, for the universal mind is omnipresent. You do not try to send out thoughts or hold a thought. Your treatment is a conscious movement of thought. As you become conscious of the qualities of health, well-being, and relaxation, these qualities will be resurgent in the experience of your mother. Results will follow.

Here is an actual example of what is misleadingly called absent treatment. A woman in Los Angeles learned that her mother in New York had suffered a coronary thrombosis. She could not go to her mother's side, but she prayed as follows:

The healing presence is right where my mother is. Her bodily condition is but a reflection of her thought-life, like shadows cast on the screen. I know that in order to change the images on the screen I must change what they reflect. I now project in my own mind the image of wholeness, harmony, and perfect health for my mother.

The Infinite Healing Presence that created my mother's body and all her organs is now saturating every atom of her being, and a river of peace flows through every cell of her body. The doctors are divinely guided and directed, and whoever touches my mother is guided to do the right thing.

I know that disease has no ultimate reality; if it had, no one could be healed. I now align myself with the infinite principle of love and life, and I know and decree that harmony, health, and peace are now being expressed in my mother's body.

She prayed in this manner several times a day. After a few days, her mother had a remarkable recovery. Her cardiologist was amazed and complimented her on her great faith in the power of God.

The conclusion arrived at in the daughter's mind and accepted by her with perfect faith set in motion the creative energy within the universal subconscious mind. This manifested itself through her mother's body as perfect health and harmony. What the daughter felt as true about her mother was simultaneously expressed in the experience of her mother.

Releasing the Kinetic Action of the Subconscious Mind

A psychologist friend of mine told me that a biopsy had shown the presence of cancerous cells in a vital organ. Her oncologist recommended a painful and dangerous treatment. Before agreeing, my friend tried another approach. Every night before going to sleep she quietly affirmed, "Every cell, nerve, tissue, and organ is now being made whole, pure, and perfect. My whole body is being restored to health and harmony."

A complete healing followed in about a month's time. Subsequent tests showed that the cancerous cells were no longer present.

I was very impressed by this, but also curious. I asked her why she repeated her affirmation prior to sleep. She told me, "Once it is set in motion in a certain direction, the kinetic action of the subconscious mind continues throughout your sleep. That is why it is so critical to give the subconscious mind something beneficial to work on as you drop off into slumber."

This was a very wise answer. Notice also that in thinking of harmony and perfect health, she never referred to her condition by name.

I strongly suggest that you stop talking about your ailments or giving them a name, especially in the hours leading up to sleep. The only sap from which they draw life is your attention and fear of them. Like the above-mentioned psychologist, become a mental surgeon. Then your troubles will be cut off the way dead branches are pruned from a tree.

On the other hand, if you are constantly naming your aches and symptoms and discussing them, you give them power over you. You inhibit the kinetic action that releases the healing power and energy of your subconscious mind. Furthermore, by the law of your own mind, these imaginings tend to take shape, *as the thing I greatly feared*. Fill your mind with the great truths of life and walk forward in the light of love.

IDEAS TO REMEMBER

1. Find out what it is that heals you. Realize that correct directions given to your subconscious mind will heal your mind and body.

2. Develop a definite plan for turning over your requests or desires to your subconscious mind.

3. Imagine the end desired and feel its reality. Follow it through, and you will get definite results.

4. Decide what belief is. Know that belief is a thought in your mind and that what you think you create.

5. It is foolish to believe in sickness or in anything that will

hurt or harm you. Believe in perfect health, prosperity, peace, wealth, and divine guidance.

6. Great and noble thoughts upon which you habitually dwell become great acts.

7. Apply the power of prayer therapy in your life. Choose a certain plan, idea, or mental picture. Unite mentally and emotionally with that idea. As you remain faithful to your mental attitude, your prayer will be answered.

8. Always remember, if you really want the power to heal, you can have it through faith, which means knowledge of the working of your conscious and subconscious mind. Faith comes with understanding.

9. Blind faith means that a person may get results in healing without any scientific understanding of the powers and forces involved.

10. Learn to pray for your loved ones who may be ill. Quiet your mind. Your thoughts of health, vitality, and perfection operating through the one universal subjective mind will be felt and made manifest in the mind of your loved one.

You avoid conflict between your conscious and subconscious in the sleepy state. Imagine the fulfillment of your desire over and over again prior to sleep. Sleep in peace and wake in joy.

Chapter Six

Practical Techniques in Mental Healings

The Law of Life is the Law of Belief. A belief is the thought in your mind. Do not believe in things that harm or hurt you. Believe in the power of your subconscious to heal, inspire, strengthen, and prosper you. According to your belief, it is done to you.

When an engineer sets out to build a bridge or design a spacecraft, he or she approaches the problem with a known, familiar technique and a set of practiced skills and methods. These techniques, skills, and methods must be learned. In the same way, there are recognized techniques, skills, and methods for governing, controlling, and directing your life. These methods and techniques are primary.

In building the Golden Gate Bridge, the engineers first had to understand mathematical principles, stresses, and strains. Second, they developed in their minds a visualization of the ideal bridge across the bay. The third step was the application of tried and proven methods by which the principles were implemented. When these three steps were completed, the bridge took form and generations of motorists began to drive across it.

If you want your prayers to be answered, you must start with the proper techniques and methods. The way in which your prayer is answered is a scientific way. Nothing happens by chance. This is a world of order and laws. In this chapter you will find practical techniques for the unfolding and nurturing of your spiritual life. Your prayers must not remain up in the air like a balloon. They must go somewhere and accomplish something in your life.

When we analyze prayer, we discover there are many different approaches and methods. We will not consider in this book the formal, ritual prayers used in religious services. These have an important place in group worship, but that is not our focus here. We are immediately concerned with effective methods of *personal* prayer that can be applied in your daily life and used to help yourself and others.

Prayer is the formulation of an idea concerning something we wish to accomplish. Prayer is the soul's sincere desire. Your desire *is* your prayer. It comes out of your deepest needs, and it reveals the things you want in life. *Blessed are they which do hunger and thirst after righteousness: for they shall be filled.* That is the real nature of prayer, the effective expression of life's hunger and thirst for peace, harmony, health, joy, and all the other blessings of life.

The Passing-Over Technique

As we have seen, the secret of effective prayer is to imbue the subconscious mind with the desired outcome. One of the simplest ways to do this is what is called the *passing-over technique*. This consists essentially of inducing the subconscious mind to take over your request by the concerted action of the conscious mind. This passing-over is best accomplished in a dreamlike state.

Know that in your deeper mind is Infinite Intelligence and Infinite Power. Just calmly think over what you want; visualize its coming into fuller fruition from this moment forward. Be like the little girl who had a very bad cough and a sore throat. She declared firmly and repeatedly, "It is passing away now. It is passing away now." It passed away in about an hour.

Your Subconscious Will Accept Your Blueprint

If you were building a new home for yourself and your family, you would take an intense interest in the blueprint for your home. You would want to make sure that the builders followed your blueprint to the last detail. You would keep watch over the materials they used. Knowing that the future life of your home depends on the quality of the materials used to construct it, you would select only the best cement, insulation, electrical wiring, roofing, and so on.

Does it not make sense to take the same care with your mental home and your mental blueprint for happiness and abundance?

All your experiences and everything that enters into your life depend upon the nature of the mental building blocks that you use in the construction of your mental home. If your blueprint is full of mental patterns of fear, worry, anxiety, or lack, and if you are despondent, doubtful, and cynical, then the quality of the mental materials you are installing in your mind will come forth as more toil, care, tension, anxiety, and limitation of all kinds.

The most fundamental and the most far-reaching activity in life is that which you build into your mentality every waking hour. Your word is silent and invisible; nevertheless, it is real.

You are building your mental home all the time, and your thoughts and mental imagery represent your blueprint. Hour by hour, moment by moment, you can build radiant health, success, and happiness by the thoughts you think, the ideas you harbor, the beliefs you accept, and the scenes you rehearse in the hidden studio of your mind. This stately mansion, upon the construction of which you are perpetually engaged, is your personality, your identity in this plane, your whole life story on this earth.

Get a new blueprint; build silently by realizing peace, harmony, joy, and goodwill in the present moment. By dwelling upon these things and claiming them, your subconscious will accept your blueprint and bring all these things to pass: *By their fruits ye shall know them.*

The Science and Art of True Prayer

The term *science* means a body of knowledge that is coordinated, arranged, and systematized. Let us think more closely about the science and art of true prayer. This body of knowledge deals with the fundamental principles of life. It describes techniques and processes that can be demonstrated in your life and in the life of any human being who applies them faithfully. The art is your technique or process, and the science behind it, is the definite response of creative mind to your mental picture or thought.

> *Ask, and you will receive; seek, and you will find;*
> *knock, and the door will be opened.* (Matthew 7:7)

What does this celebrated verse tell us? It clearly means that you shall receive that for which you ask. It shall be opened to you when you knock, and you shall find that for which you are searching. This teaching implies the definiteness of mental and spiritual laws. There is always a direct response from the Infinite

Intelligence of your subconscious mind to your conscious thinking. If you ask for bread, you will not receive a stone.

You must ask *believing,* if you are to receive. Your mind moves from the thought to the thing. Unless there is first an image in the mind, it cannot move, for there would be nothing for it to move toward. Your prayer, which is your mental act, must be accepted as an image in your mind before the power from your subconscious will play upon it and make it productive. You must reach a point of acceptance in your mind, an unqualified and undisputed state of agreement.

This contemplation should be accompanied by a feeling of joy and restfulness in foreseeing the certain accomplishment of your desire. The sound basis for the art and science of true prayer is your knowledge and complete confidence that the movement of your conscious mind will gain a definite response from your subconscious mind, which has Boundless Wisdom and Infinite Power. By following this procedure, your prayers will be answered.

All frustration is due to unfulfilled desires. If you dwell on obstacles, delays, and difficulties, your subconscious mind responds accordingly, and you are blocking your own good.

You can build radiant health, success, and happiness by the thoughts you think in the hidden studio of your mind.

Desire to do things the easy way with the sure aid of mental science.

The Visualization Technique

The easiest and most obvious way to formulate an idea is to visualize it, to see it in your mind's eye as vividly as if it were alive. You can see with the naked eye only what already exists in the external world. In a similar way, that which you can visualize in your mind's eye already exists in the invisible realms of your mind. Any picture you have in your mind is the substance of things hoped for and the evidence of things not seen. What you form in your imagination is as real as any part of your body. The idea and the thought are real and will one day appear in your objective world if you are faithful to your mental image.

This process of thinking forms impressions in your mind. These impressions in turn become manifested as facts and experiences in your life. Architects visualize the type of building they want. They see it as they desire it to be when completed. Their imagery and thought-processes become a plastic mold from which the building will emerge. It may be beautiful or ugly, a skyscraper or a one-story shack, but it begins as a visualization. The architect's mental imagery is projected as it is drawn on paper. Eventually, the contractor and construction workers gather the essential materials, and the building progresses until it stands finished, conforming perfectly to the mental patterns of the architect.

I always use the visualization technique before I speak to an audience. I quiet the wheels of my mind so that I may present to the subconscious mind my images of thought. Then I picture the entire auditorium. Its seats are filled with men and women who are all illumined and inspired by the Infinite Healing Presence within each one. I *see* them as radiant, happy, and free.

Having first built up the idea in my imagination, I quietly sustain it there as a mental picture while I imagine I hear people saying, "I am healed," "I feel wonderful," "I am transformed." I keep this up for ten minutes or more. I let myself know and feel that each person's mind and body are saturated with love, wholeness, beauty, and perfection. My awareness grows to the point where in my mind I can hear the voices of the multitude proclaiming their health and happiness. Then I release the whole picture and go on the platform.

Almost every time I speak, having used this technique, some people stop by afterward to tell me their prayers were answered.

Mental-Movie Method

As the old saying proclaims, "A picture is worth a thousand words." The fact must be stressed that the subconscious mind will bring to pass any picture held in the mind and backed by faith: *Act as though I am, and I will be.*

A number of years ago I was in the Midwest on a lecture tour that took me to several states. I wanted to have a permanent base in the area so that I could serve those who needed my help. My travels carried me far away, but I did not forget the idea of a permanent base. One evening in Spokane, Washington, I relaxed on a couch in my hotel room. I immobilized my attention. In a quiet, passive manner I imagined that I was talking to a large audience. I said to those listening, "I am glad to be here; I have prayed for this ideal opportunity."

I saw that imaginary audience in my mind's eye, and I felt the reality of it all. I played the role of the actor and dramatized this mental movie. I felt satisfied that this picture was being conveyed to my subconscious mind, which would bring it to pass in its own way. The next morning, on awakening, I felt a great sense of peace and satisfaction. A few days later I received a call from an organization in the Midwest, asking me to take over as director. I did so, and I enjoyed several years of deeply fulfilling work there.

The method I have just described is often referred to as "the mental-movie method." I have received a great many letters from people who have read my books or heard me speak, telling me of the wonderful results they have obtained by using this technique.

One area in which the mental-movie method seems especially useful is in selling property. If you have a home or property for sale, I suggest that you first satisfy yourself in your own mind that your price is right and fair to both you and the eventual buyer. After having done this, quiet your mind, relax, let go, and get into a drowsy, sleepy state that reduces all mental effort to a minimum. Now picture the check in your hands, rejoice in the check, give thanks for the check, and go off to sleep feeling the naturalness of the whole mental movie created in your mind.

You must act as if this is already an objective reality. When you do, the subconscious mind will take it as an impression. Then, the Infinite Intelligence will draw to you the buyer who really wants to have the property and who will love it and prosper in it. Through the deeper currents of the mind, the buyer and the seller are brought together. A mental picture held in the mind, backed by faith, will come to pass.

The Baudoin Technique

Charles Baudoin was a professor at the Rousseau Institute in France. He was a brilliant psychotherapist and a research director of the New Nancy School of Healing. He discovered that the best way to impress the subconscious mind was to enter into a drowsy, sleepy state, or a state akin to sleep, in which all effort was reduced to a minimum. Then the idea can be conveyed to the subconscious in a quiet, passive, receptive way, by reflection.

As Baudoin explained:

A very simple way of securing this [impregnation of the subconscious mind] is to condense the idea which is to be the object of suggestion, to sum it up in a brief phrase which can be readily graven on the memory, and to repeat it over and over again as a lullaby.

A few years ago, a young widow in Los Angeles found herself caught up in a prolonged and bitter family dispute. Her late husband had left his entire estate to her, but his sons and daughters from a previous marriage had filed suit to break the will. Her offers of a settlement were spurned.

When she asked me for my help, I explained the Baudoin technique to her. I urged her to condense the idea of her need into a phrase of a few words that could be easily impressed on her memory. The phrase she found was "It is finished in divine order." To her, these words meant that Infinite Intelligence, operating through the laws of her subconscious mind, would bring about a harmonious conclusion through the principle of harmony.

Every night for ten nights she sat in an armchair, systematically relaxed her body, and entered into the sleepy state. Once in a sleepy state, she affirmed slowly, quietly, and feelingly the statement, "It is finished in divine order," over and over again. She found herself achieving a sense of inner peace and an all-pervading tranquillity; then she went off into her deep, normal sleep.

On the morning of the eleventh day, she woke up with a sense of well-being and a conviction that it was indeed finished. Her attorney called her that same day. The opposing attorney and his clients were willing to settle. A harmonious agreement was reached, and the lawsuit was dropped.

The Sleeping Technique

When you enter into a sleepy, drowsy state, effort is reduced to a minimum. The conscious mind is submerged to a great extent when in a sleepy state. The reason for this is that the highest degree of outcropping of the subconscious occurs just prior to sleep and just after you awaken. In this state the negative thoughts, which tend to neutralize your desire and so prevent acceptance by your subconscious mind, are no longer present.

Suppose you want to get rid of a destructive habit. Assume a comfortable posture, relax your body, and be still. Get into a sleepy state, and in that sleepy state, say quietly, over and over as a lullaby, "I am completely free from this habit; harmony and peace of mind reign supreme." Repeat these words slowly, quietly, and lovingly for five or ten minutes night and morning. Each time you repeat the words the emotional value becomes greater. When the urge comes to repeat the negative habit, repeat this formula out loud to yourself. By this means you induce the subconscious to accept the idea, and a healing follows.

The "Thank You" Technique

In the Bible, Paul recommends that we make known our requests with praise and thanksgiving. Some extraordinary results follow this simple method of prayer. The thankful heart is always close to the creative forces of the universe, causing countless blessings to flow toward it by the law of reciprocal relationship, based on a cosmic law of action and reaction.

Recently a young mother told me of her experience with this technique. She said, "I was out of work and broke, with three small children to feed and clothe. I didn't know where to turn. Then I heard you explain that we should be thankful even before our prayers are answered. It was as if a light had gone on in my mind. I knew I had to try it."

Every night and morning for about three weeks, this woman repeated the words, "Thank you, Father, for my wealth." She did this in a relaxed, peaceful manner and continued until the feeling or mood of thankfulness dominated her mind. She imagined she was addressing the Infinite Power and Intelligence within, though she knew, of course, that she could not literally see the creative intelligence or Infinite Mind. She was seeing with the inner eye of spiritual perception, realizing that her thought-image of wealth was the first cause, relative to the money, position, and food she needed. Her thought-feeling was the substance of wealth, untrammeled by antecedent conditions of any kind.

By repeating, "Thank you, Father," over and over, the woman's mind and heart were lifted up to the point of acceptance. When thoughts of lack, poverty, and distress came into her mind, she would say again, "Thank you, Father," as often as necessary. She knew that as she kept up the thankful attitude, she would recondition her mind to the idea of wealth. This is exactly what happened.

This mother's prayer had an interesting sequel. Shortly after she began to pray in the way just described, she met a former employer on the street whom she had not seen in five years. The former employer offered her a responsible, well-paid position. He even advanced her a temporary loan to tide her over until her first paycheck. As she said to me, "I'll never forget the amazing power of 'Thank you, Father.' It has worked wonders for me."

The Affirmative Method
The effectiveness of an affirmation is determined largely by your understanding of the truth and meaning that underlie the words *In praying use not vain repetition*. The power of your affirmation lies in the intelligent application of definite and specific positives. Suppose a schoolchild adds three and three and puts down seven on the blackboard. The teacher affirms with

mathematical certainty that three and three are six; therefore, the child changes the figures accordingly. The teacher's statement did not *make* three and three equal six. This was already a mathematical truth that in turn caused the child to rearrange the figures on the blackboard.

It is abnormal to be sick; it is normal to be healthy. Health is the truth of your being. When you affirm health, harmony, and peace for yourself or another, and when you realize these are universal principles of your own being, you rearrange the negative patterns of your subconscious mind based on your faith and understanding of that which you affirm.

The result of the affirmative process of prayer depends on conforming to the principles of life, regardless of appearances. Consider for a moment: There is a principle of mathematics but none of error. There is a principle of truth but none of dishonesty. There is a principle of intelligence but none of ignorance. There is a principle of harmony but none of discord. There is a principle of health but none of disease, and there is a principle of abundance but none of poverty.

I chose to use the affirmative method when my sister was about to be operated on for the removal of gallstones in a hospital in England. Her diagnosis was based on the usual hospital tests and X-ray procedures. She asked me to pray for her recovery. I was over six thousand miles away, but this did not disturb me. There is no time or space in the mind principle. Infinite Mind or Intelligence is present in its entirety at every point simultaneously.

Several times a day I withdrew all thought from the contemplation of my sister's symptoms and from the corporeal personality altogether. Calmly, confidently, I affirmed as follows:

This prayer is for my sister Catherine. She is relaxed and at peace, poised, balanced, serene, and calm. The healing intelligence of her subconscious mind that created her body is now transforming every cell, nerve, tissue, muscle, and bone of her being according to the perfect pattern of all organs lodged in her subconscious mind. Silently, quietly, all distorted thought patterns in her subconscious mind are removed and dissolved, and the vitality, wholeness, and beauty of the life-principle are made manifest in every atom of her being. She is now open and receptive to the healing currents that are flowing through her like a river, restoring her to perfect health, harmony, and peace. All distortions and ugly images are now washed away by the infinite ocean of love and peace flowing through her, and it is so.

At the end of two weeks, my sister had another examination. Her X-rays were negative. Her doctor admitted that she showed a remarkable healing and called off the scheduled surgery.

To affirm is to state that it is so. As you maintain this attitude of mind as true, regardless of all evidence to the contrary, you will receive an answer to your prayer. Your thought can only affirm, for even if you deny something, you are actually affirming the presence of what you deny. Repeating an affirmation, knowing what you are saying and why you are saying it, leads the mind to that state of consciousness where it accepts that which you state as true. Keep on affirming the truths of life until you get the subconscious reaction that satisfies.

The Argumentative Method

This method is just what its name implies. It stems from the amazing work of Dr. Phineas Parkhurst Quimby, a pioneer in mental and spiritual healing who lived and practiced in Belfast,

Maine, over a century ago. He was really the father of psycho-somatic medicine and the first psychoanalyst. He also had a re-markable capacity to diagnose clairvoyantly the cause of the patient's trouble, pains, and aches.

In brief, the argumentative method as employed so success-fully by Quimby consists of spiritual reasoning. You convince the patient and yourself that the sickness is due to false beliefs, groundless fears, and negative patterns lodged in the subcon-scious mind. You reason it out clearly in your mind and con-vince your patient that the disease or ailment is due only to a distorted, twisted pattern of thought that has taken form in the body. This wrong belief in some external power and external causes has now externalized itself as sickness and can be changed by changing the thought patterns.

You explain to the sick person that the basis of all healing is a change of belief. You also point out that the subconscious mind created the body and all its organs; therefore, it knows how to heal it, can heal it, and is doing so now as you speak. You argue in the courtroom of your mind that the disease is a shadow of the mind based on disease-soaked, morbid thought-imagery. You continue to build up all the evidence you can muster on behalf of the healing power within, which cre-ated all the organs in the first place, and which has a perfect pattern of every cell, nerve, and tissue within it.

Then, you render a verdict in the courthouse of your mind in favor of yourself and your patient. You liberate the sick one by faith and spiritual understanding. Your mental and spiritual evidence is overwhelming. Since there is but one mind, what you feel as true is made manifest in the experience of the pa-tient, and a healing follows.

The Absolute Method Is Like Modern Ultrasound Therapy

Many people throughout the world practice this form of prayer treatment with wonderful results. The person using the absolute method mentions the name of the patient. Then she silently thinks of God and his qualities and attributes, such as, God is All Bliss, Boundless Love, Infinite Intelligence, All-Powerful, Boundless Wisdom, Absolute Harmony, Indescribable Beauty, and Perfection. As she quietly thinks along these lines her consciousness is lifted into a new spiritual dimension. She feels the infinite ocean of God's love dissolving everything unlike itself in the mind and body of the patient for whom she is praying. She feels all the power and love of God is now focused on the patient. Whatever is bothersome or vexing is now completely neutralized in the presence of the infinite ocean of life and love.

The absolute method of prayer might be compared to the latest developments in ultrasound therapy. These were explained to me recently by a distinguished physician in Los Angeles. The device she uses in her work generates powerful sound waves at extremely high frequencies. When these are focused on areas of the body where there are abnormal tissues, the affected cells resonate to the ultrasound and respond to it.

To the degree that we rise in consciousness by contemplating the qualities and attributes of God, we generate spiritual waves of harmony, health, and peace. Those on whom these waves are focused then resonate to them and respond. Many remarkable healings have been achieved by this technique of prayer.

A Crippled Woman Walks

Dr. Quimby often used the absolute method in the later years of his healing career.

One of his manuscripts describes how he healed a crippled woman. He was called on to visit this woman, who was lame, aged, and bedridden. He states that her ailment was due to the fact that she was imprisoned by a creed so small and contracted that she could not stand upright and move about. She was living in the tomb of fear and ignorance. Because she took the Bible literally, it frightened her.

"In this tomb," Quimby said, "was the presence and power of God trying to burst the bands, break through the bonds, and rise from the dead."

When the woman would ask others for an explanation of some passage of the Bible, the answer would be a stone; then she would hunger for the bread of life. Dr. Quimby diagnosed her case as a mind cloudy and stagnated due to excitation and fear, caused by the inability to see clearly the meaning of the passage of the Bible that she had been reading. This showed itself in her body by the heavy and sluggish feeling that would terminate as paralysis.

At this point Quimby asked her what was meant in the Bible verses:

> For a little longer I shall be with you; then I am going
> away to him who sent me. You will look for me, but
> you will not find me. Where I am, you cannot come.
> (John 7:33–34)

She replied that it meant Jesus went to heaven. Quimby explained what it really meant by telling her that Jesus would *be with her a little while* was his explanation of her symptoms, feelings, and their causes. He had compassion and sympathy for her momentarily, but he could not remain in that mental state. The next step was *to go to him that sent us*. This, Quimby pointed out, was the creative power of God in all of us.

Quimby immediately traveled in his mind and contemplated the divine ideal; that is, the vitality, intelligence, harmony, and power of God functioning in the sick person. This is why he said to the woman, "Therefore, where I go you cannot come, for you are in your narrow, restricted belief, and I am in health."

This prayer and explanation produced an instantaneous sensation, and a change came over her mind. She walked without her crutches! Quimby said it was one of the most singular of all his healings. She was, as it were, dead to error, and to bring her to life or truth was to raise her from the dead. Quimby quoted the resurrection of Christ and applied it to her own Christ or health; this produced a powerful effect on her. He also explained to her that the truth that she accepted was the angel or idea that rolled away the stone of fear, ignorance, and superstition. This then released the healing power of God, which made her whole.

The Decree Method

Power goes into our word according to the feeling and faith behind it. When we realize the power that moves the world is moving on our behalf and is backing up our word, our confidence and assurance grow. You do not try to add power to power. There must be no mental striving, coercion, force, or mental wrestling.

A young woman used the decree method on a young man who was constantly phoning her, pressing her for dates. She found it very difficult to get rid of him. When he began to show up at her workplace, she realized that she had to do something drastic at once.

Several times a day, she put herself into a quiet state and repeatedly decreed as follows:

I release J———R———unto God. He is in his true place at all times. I am free, and he is free. I now decree that my words go forth into infinite mind and it brings it to pass. It is so.

According to her, the young man immediately disappeared from her life. She has never seen him since. She says, "It was as if the ground swallowed him up."

In all your designs you will succeed, and light will shine on your path. (Job 22:28)

IDEAS TO REMEMBER

1. Be a mental engineer and use tried and proven techniques in building a grander and greater life.

2. Your desire is your prayer. Picture the fulfillment of your desire now and feel its reality, and you will experience the joy of the answered prayer.

3. Desire to accomplish things the easy way—with the sure aid of mental science.

4. You can build radiant health, success, and happiness by the thoughts you think in the hidden studio of your mind.

5. Experiment scientifically until you personally prove that there is always a direct response from the Infinite Intelligence of your subconscious mind to your conscious thinking.

6. Feel the joy and restfulness in foreseeing the certain accomplishment of your desire. Any mental picture you have in your mind is the substance of things hoped for and the evidence of things not seen.

7. A mental picture is worth a thousand words. Your subconscious will bring to pass any picture held in the mind backed by faith.

8. Avoid all effort or mental coercion in prayer. Get into a sleepy, drowsy state and lull yourself to sleep feeling and knowing that your prayer is answered.

9. Remember that the thankful heart is always close to the riches of the universe.

10. To affirm is to state that it is so, and as you maintain this attitude of mind as true, regardless of all evidence to the contrary, you will receive an answer to your prayer.

11. Generate waves of harmony, health, and peace by thinking of the love and the glory of God.

12. What you decree and feel as true will come to pass. Decree harmony, health, peace, and abundance.

What you consciously affirm, you must not mentally deny a few moments later. This will neutralize the good that you have affirmed.

Chapter Seven

The Tendency of the Subconscious Mind Is Lifeward

The treasure house is within you. Look within for the answer your heart desires.

More than 90 percent of your mental life is subconscious. If you fail to make use of this marvelous power, you condemn yourself to live within very narrow limits.

Your subconscious processes are always lifeward and constructive. Your subconscious is the builder of your body and maintains all its vital functions. It is on the job twenty-four hours a day and never sleeps. It is always trying to help and preserve you from harm.

Your subconscious mind is in touch with Infinite Life and Boundless Wisdom, and its impulses and ideas are always lifeward. The great aspirations, inspirations, and visions for a grander and nobler life spring from the subconscious. Your profoundest convictions are those you cannot argue about rationally because they do not come from your conscious mind; they come from your subconscious mind.

Your subconscious speaks to you in intuitions, impulses, hunches, intimations, urges, and ideas. It is always telling you to rise, transcend, grow, advance, adventure, and move forward to greater heights. The urge to love, to save the lives of others, comes from the depths of your subconscious. For example, during the great San Francisco earthquake and fire of April 18, 1906, invalids and handicapped people who had been confined to bed for long periods of time rose up and performed amazing feats of bravery and endurance. The intense desire welled up within them to save others at all costs, and their subconscious responded accordingly.

Great artists, musicians, poets, speakers, and writers tune in with their subconscious powers and become animated and inspired. Robert Louis Stevenson, before he went to sleep, used to charge his subconscious with the task of evolving stories for him while he slept. He was accustomed to ask his subconscious to give him a good, marketable thriller whenever his bank account was low. Stevenson said the intelligence of his deeper mind gave him the story piece by piece, like a serial. This shows how your subconscious will speak lofty and wise sayings through you that your conscious mind knows nothing about.

Mark Twain confided to the world on many occasions that he never worked in his life. All his humor and all his great writings were the result of his ability to tap the inexhaustible reservoir of his subconscious mind.

How the Body Portrays the Workings of the Mind

The interaction of your conscious and subconscious mind requires a similar interaction between the corresponding systems of nerves. The cerebrospinal or voluntary system is the organ of the conscious mind. The autonomic system is the organ of the subconscious mind. The voluntary nervous system is the channel through which you receive conscious perception by means of your physical senses and exercise voluntary control over the movement of your body. This system has its control center in the cerebral cortex of the brain.

The autonomic nervous system, sometimes referred to as the involuntary nervous system, has its centers of activity in other parts of the brain, including the cerebellum, the brain stem, and the amygdala. These organs have their own connections to the major systems of the body and support their vital functions even when conscious awareness is absent.

The two systems may work separately or synchronously. For example, when a perception of danger arrives at the switching center in the cerebellum, messages are sent both to the conscious cortex and to the subconscious amygdala. The person's defensive abilities may start to respond to the danger even before the danger is consciously noticed and evaluated.

A simple way of looking at the mental and physical interaction is to realize that your conscious mind grasps an idea that is parallel to a corresponding series of electrical impulses in your voluntary system of nerves. This in turn causes a similar current to be generated in your involuntary system of nerves, thus handing the idea over to your subconscious mind, which is the creative medium. This is how your thoughts become things.

Every thought entertained by your conscious mind and accepted as true is sent by your cortex to the other organs of the brain that support your subconscious mind, to be made into your flesh and to be brought forth into your world as a reality.

An Intelligence That Takes Care of the Body
When you study the cellular system and the structure of the organs, such as eyes, ears, heart, liver, bladder, and so on, you discover that they consist of groups of cells that form a group

intelligence that allows them to function together. They are able to take orders and carry them out in deductive function at the suggestion of the master mind (conscious mind).

A careful study of the single-celled organism shows you what goes on in your complex body. Though the single-celled organism has no organs, it still gives evidence of mind action and reaction performing the basic functions of movement, alimentation, assimilation, and elimination.

Many say there is an intelligence that will take care of your body if you let it alone. This is true in a sense. The difficulty is that the conscious mind always interferes with its sensory evidence based on outer appearances. These lead to the sway of false beliefs, fears, and mere opinion. When fears, false beliefs, and negative patterns are made to register in your subconscious mind through psychological, emotional conditioning, there is no other course open to the subconscious mind except to act on the blueprint specifications offered it.

The Subconscious Mind Works Continually for the Common Good

The subjective self within you works continuously for the general good, reflecting an innate principle of harmony behind all things. Your subconscious mind has its own will, and it is very real in itself. It functions night and day, whether you will it or not. It is the builder of your body, but you cannot see, hear, or feel it building. All this is a silent process. Your subconscious has a life of its own that is always moving toward harmony, health, and peace. This is the divine norm within it, seeking expression through you at all times.

The great secret possessed by the great men of all ages was their ability to contact and release the powers of their subconscious mind. You can do the same.

Be a mental engineer and use tried-and-true techniques in build-
ing a greater and grander life.

How Humans Interfere with the Innate Principle of Harmony

To think correctly, scientifically, we must know the "Truth." As the ancient saying puts it, "Ye shall know the truth, and the truth shall set you free." To know the truth is to be in harmony with the Infinite Intelligence and Power of your subconscious mind, which is always moving lifeward.

Every thought or action that is not harmonious, whether through ignorance or design, will result in discord and limitation of all kinds.

Scientists inform us that you build a new body every eleven months; so from a physical standpoint you are really only eleven months old. If you build defects back into your body by thoughts of fear, anger, jealousy, and ill will, you have no one to blame but yourself.

You are the sum total of your own thoughts. You can keep from entertaining negative thought and imagery. The way to get rid of darkness is with light; the way to overcome cold is with heat; the way to overcome the negative thought is to substitute the good thought. Affirm the good, and the bad will vanish.

Why It's Normal to Be Healthy, Vital, and Strong

The average child born into the world is perfectly healthy, with all its organs functioning perfectly. This is the normal state, and we should remain healthy, vital, and strong. The instinct of self-preservation is the strongest instinct of your nature, and it constitutes a most potent, ever present, and constantly operative truth, inherent in your nature. All your thoughts, ideas, and beliefs must operate with greater potentiality when they are in harmony with the innate life-principle in you, which is forever seeking to preserve and protect you along all lines. It follows from this that normal conditions can be restored with greater ease and certainty than abnormal conditions can be induced.

It is abnormal to be sick. The condition of sickness simply means you are going against the stream of life and thinking negatively. The law of life is the law of growth; all nature testifies to the operation of this law by silently, constantly expressing itself in growth. Where there is growth and expression, there must be life; where there is life there must be harmony; and where there is harmony, there is perfect health.

If your thought is in harmony with the creative principle of your subconscious mind, you are in tune with the innate principle of harmony. If you entertain thoughts that are not in accordance with the principle of harmony, these thoughts cling to you, harass you, worry you, and finally bring about disease, and if persisted in, possibly death.

In the healing of disease, you must increase the inflow and distribution of the vital forces of your subconscious mind throughout your system. This can be done by eliminating thoughts of fear, worry, anxiety, jealousy, hatred, and every other destructive thought. These tend to tear down and destroy your nerves and glands—body tissue that controls the elimination of all waste material and keeps the organism in a state of purity.

Pott's Disease Cured

Pott's disease, or tuberculosis of the spine, used to be a terrible scourge of children. One child who contracted it was named Frederick Elias Andrews, of Indianapolis, Indiana. The disease made him a twisted cripple who could not walk and had to go about on his hands and knees. His physician pronounced him incurable. Andrews refused to accept that verdict. He began to pray. He created his own affirmation, repeating it over and over many times a day and mentally absorbing the qualities he needed:

I am whole, perfect, strong, powerful, loving, harmonious, and happy.

He made this prayer the last utterance on his lips at night and the first in the morning. He prayed for others as well, sending out thoughts of love and health.

This attitude of mind and way of prayer returned to him multiplied many times. His faith and perseverance paid off with big dividends. When thoughts of fear, anger, jealousy, or envy drew his attention, he would immediately start his counteracting force of affirmation going in his mind. His subconscious mind responded according to the nature of his habitual thinking. He became a strong, straight, well-formed man.

This is the meaning of the statement in the Bible:

Go; your faith has cured you. (Mark 10:52)

How Faith in Your Subconscious Makes You Whole

A young man who had severe eye trouble came to my lectures on the healing power of the subconscious mind. His ophthalmologist told him he would have to have a delicate, risky operation. After learning about the scientific basis of prayer, the young man said to himself, "My subconscious made my eyes, and it can heal me."

Each night, as he went to sleep, he entered into a drowsy,

meditative state, the condition akin to sleep. His attention was immobilized and focused on the eye doctor. He imagined the doctor was in front of him, and he plainly heard, or imagined he heard, the doctor saying to him, "A miracle has happened!" He heard this over and over again every night for five minutes or so before going to sleep.

Three weeks later he had another appointment with the ophthalmologist who had examined his eyes. The physician examined him again, then exclaimed, "This is a miracle!"

What had happened? This man impressed his subconscious mind, using the eye doctor as an instrument or means of convincing it and conveying the idea. Through repetition, faith, and expectancy he impregnated his subconscious mind. His subconscious mind had made his eye. It held within it the perfect pattern or blueprint of the eye's normal, healthy structure. Once impregnated with the idea of restoring the eye to its healthy state, it immediately proceeded to heal the eye. This is another example of how faith in the healing power of your subconscious can make you whole.

IDEAS TO REMEMBER

1. Your subconscious is the builder of your body and is on the job twenty-four hours a day. You interfere with its life-giving pattern by negative thinking.

2. Charge your subconscious with the task of evolving an answer to any problem, prior to sleep, and it will answer you.

3. Watch your thoughts. Every thought accepted as true is sent by your conscious cortex to your subconscious brain structures and is brought into your world as a reality.

4. Know that you can remake yourself by giving a new blueprint to your subconscious mind.

5. The tendency of your subconscious is always lifeward. Your job is with your conscious mind. Feed your subconscious mind with premises that are true. Your subconscious is always reproducing according to your habitual mental patterns.

6. You build a new body every eleven months. Change your body by changing your thoughts and keeping them changed.

7. It is normal to be healthy. It is abnormal to be ill. There is within the innate principle of harmony.

8. Thoughts of jealousy, fear, worry, and anxiety tear down and destroy your nerves and glands, bringing about mental and physical diseases of all kinds.

What you affirm consciously and feel as true will be made manifest in your mind, body, and affairs. Affirm the good and enter into the joy of living.

Chapter Eight

How to Get the Results You Want

The action in your thought and the reaction in your response is the response of your subconscious mind. If you think wise your decisions will be wise.

Not all prayers are answered. Everyone knows that. Skeptics see this as evidence that prayer does not work. What they overlook is that for prayer to work, it must be used effectively, with a clear understanding of its scientific basis. Only then can we know why a particular prayer was not effective and arrive at a practical method to make it more effective.

What if you find your prayers are not answered as you would like? You must understand the principal reasons for such a failure. These are: lack of confidence or too much effort. Many people block answers to their prayers by failing to fully comprehend the workings of their subconscious mind. When you know how your mind functions, you gain a measure of confidence.

You must remember that whenever your subconscious mind accepts an idea, it immediately begins to execute it. It uses all its mighty resources to that end. It mobilizes all the mental and spiritual laws of your deeper mind. This law is true for good ideas, but it holds true for bad ideas as well. Consequently, if you use your subconscious mind negatively, it brings trouble, failure, and confusion. When you use it constructively, it brings guidance, freedom, and peace of mind.

The right answer is inevitable when your thoughts are positive, constructive, and loving. From this it is obvious that the only thing you have to do in order to overcome failure is to get your subconscious to accept your idea or request. Feel its reality now and the law of your mind will do the rest. Turn over your request with faith and confidence, and your subconscious will take over and answer for you.

Any time you try to force your subconscious mind to do something for you, you will fail. The results you want will become more distant instead of closer. Your subconscious mind does not respond to mental coercion. It responds to your faith or conscious mind acceptance.

Your failure to get results may also be a consequence of mentally making such statements as:

- Things are getting worse.

- I will never get an answer.

- I see no way out.

- It is hopeless.

- I don't know what to do.

- I'm all mixed up.

When you use such statements, you get no response or cooperation from your subconscious mind. Like a soldier marking time, you go neither forward nor backward. In other words, you don't get anywhere.

Imagine that you got into a taxi and gave the driver a half dozen different directions. He would become hopelessly confused. He might refuse to take you anywhere. Even if he tried to follow your instructions, chances are he would not be able to. Where you would end up is anybody's guess.

It is the same when working with the enormous powers of your subconscious mind. You must have a clear-cut idea in your mind. You must arrive at the definite decision that there is a way out, a solution to the vexing problem in sickness. Only the Infinite Intelligence within your subconscious knows the answer. When you come to that clear-cut conclusion in your conscious mind, your mind is then made up, and *according to your belief is it done unto you*.

Easy Does It

A homeowner whose furnace broke down during a bitter cold snap called a repairman. The repairman came at once. Within half an hour, the furnace was working again. The repairman then gave the homeowner a bill for $200.

"What!" the outraged homeowner exclaimed. "It took you no time at all. All you did was replace one small part. How can you have the nerve to charge me two hundred dollars for a little gizmo that can't be worth more than five dollars?"

The repairman shrugged. "I charged you only two dollars for the broken part," he said. "That's what I had to pay for it."

The homeowner waved the bill in his face. "Two dollars!" he yelled. "This says two hundred dollars!"

"That's right," the repairman said. "The other one hundred ninety-eight is for knowing what was wrong and how to fix it."

Your subconscious mind is the master mechanic, the all-wise

one. It knows the ways and means of healing any organ of your body. Decree health, and your subconscious will establish it, but relaxation is the key. "Easy does it."

Do not let yourself get bogged down in thinking about details and means. Know what the end result will be. Get the feel of the happy solution to your problem, whether it is health, finances, or personal relationships. Remember how you felt after you recovered from a serious illness. Bear in mind that your feeling is the touchstone of all subconscious demonstration. Your new idea must be felt subjectively in a finished state, felt not as something that may come to pass in the future, but as something that is actually coming to pass at this moment.

Use Imagination, Not Willpower

Enlisting the powers of your subconscious mind is not like pushing against an obstacle. Working harder does not lead to better results. Willpower won't do it. Instead, visualize the end and the state of freedom it produces. You will find your intellect trying to get in the way, trying to find ways to solve the problem and impose those ways on your subconscious.

Resist this. Put away your intellectual problem-solving skills. Persist in maintaining a simple, childlike, miracle-making faith. Picture yourself without the ailment or problem. Imagine the emotional gratification of the freedom state you seek. Cut out all red tape from the process. The simple way is the best.

How Disciplined Imagination Works Wonders

A wonderful way to get a response from your subconscious mind is through disciplined or scientific imagination. As we have seen, the subconscious mind is the architect and builder of the body. It controls all your vital functions.

The Bible says, *Whatsoever ye shall ask in prayer, believing, ye shall receive*. To believe is to accept something as true, to live in the state of being it. As you sustain this mood, you shall experience the joy of the answered prayer.

> *Imagination is your most powerful faculty. Imagine what is lovely and of good report. You are what you imagine yourself to be.*

> *Guidance comes as a feeling, an inner awareness, an overpowering hunch, whereby you know that you know. It is an inner sense of touch. Follow it.*

The Three Steps to Success in Prayer

Successful prayer requires three basic steps:

1. Acknowledge or admit the problem.

2. Turn the problem over to the subconscious mind, which alone knows the most effective solution or way out.

3. Rest with a sense of deep conviction that it is done.

Doubts and hesitations only weaken your prayer. Do not say to yourself, "I wish I could be healed" or "I hope this works." Your feeling about the work to be done sets the tone. Harmony is yours. Know that health is yours.

You become effective by becoming a vehicle for the Infinite Healing Power of the subconscious mind. Pass on the idea of health to your subconscious mind with complete conviction; then relax. Give yourself over to its power. Say to the condition and circumstance, "This, too, shall pass." Through relaxation and conviction, you impregnate your subconscious mind. This enables the kinetic energy behind the idea to take over and bring it into concrete realization.

Why You May Get the Opposite of What You Pray For

Emile Coué was a celebrated French psychologist whose lectures gained him many admirers and followers in the United States. One of his important insights was this:

> When your desires and imagination are in conflict, your imagination invariably gains the day.

He referred to this as the law of reverse effort.

Suppose you were asked to walk along a narrow plank that was resting on the floor. You would do it easily, without question. But now suppose the same plank were twenty feet up, stretching between two walls. Would you walk it? *Could* you?

Probably not. Your desire to walk the length of the plank would come into conflict with your imagination. You would imagine yourself toppling off the plank and falling a long way to the ground. You might very much *want* to walk across the plank, but your fear of falling would keep you from being able to do it. The more effort you put into conquering your imagination or suppressing it, the greater strength is given to the dominant idea of falling.

The thought "I will use my willpower to overcome my *failure*" reinforces the thought of failure. Mental effort often leads to self-defeat, creating the opposite of what is desired. To focus on the need to exert willpower is to emphasize the condition of powerlessness. It is like deciding that you will do all you can to not think of a green hippopotamus. The decision makes the idea of a green hippo dominate the mind, and the subconscious always responds more to the dominant idea. Your subconscious will accept the stronger of two contradictory propositions.

Maybe you find yourself thinking

• I want a healing; why can't I get it?

• I try so hard, why don't I get results?

• I must force myself to pray harder.

• I must use all the willpower I have.

You must realize where your error lies. You are trying too hard! Never try to compel the subconscious mind to accept your idea by exercising willpower. Such attempts are doomed to failure. All too often, you end up getting the opposite of what you prayed for. The effortless way is better.

Have you ever had something like this happen to you? You have to take an examination of some kind. You have put in a lot of time studying and reviewing the material. You feel as if you know it well. But when you face a blank exam page, you find that your mind is equally blank. All your knowledge of the subject has suddenly deserted you. You can't recall a single relevant thought. You grit your teeth and summon all the powers of your will, but the harder you try; the farther the knowledge seems to flee.

Frustrated, you leave the examination room. The mental pressure eases. Suddenly the answers you were hunting for so desperately a few minutes ago flow tantalizingly back into your mind. You told yourself you knew the material, and sure enough, you did . . . but not when you needed to. The mistake you made was to try to force yourself to remember. By the law of reversed effort, this led not to success, but to failure. What you got was the opposite of what you asked or prayed for.

The Conflict of Desire and Imagination Must Be Resolved

To use mental force or willpower is to presuppose that there is opposition. But the act of imagining opposition *creates* opposition. If your attention is focused on the obstacles to obtaining what you desire, it is no longer concentrating on the *means* to obtain your desire.

In the Bible, it is said:

> *If two of you agree on earth about any request you have to make, that request will be granted by my heavenly Father.* (Matthew 18:19)

Who are these two who are spoken of? They stand for the harmonious union or agreement between your conscious and subconscious on any idea, desire, or mental image. When there is no longer any quarrel between the different parts of your mind, your prayer will be answered. The two agreeing may also be represented as you and your desire, your thought and feeling, your idea and emotion, your desire and imagination.

You avoid all conflict between your desires and imagination by entering into a drowsy, sleepy state that brings all effort to a minimum. The conscious mind is submerged to a great extent when in a sleepy state. The best time to impregnate your subconscious is just prior to sleep. The reason for this is that the highest degree of outcropping of the subconscious occurs just before going to sleep and just after we awaken. In this state the negative thoughts and imagery that tend to neutralize your desire and so prevent acceptance by your subconscious mind no longer present themselves. When you imagine the reality of the fulfilled desire and feel the thrill of accomplishment, your subconscious brings about the realization of your desire.

A great many people solve all their dilemmas and problems by the play of their controlled, directed, and disciplined imagination. They know that whatever they imagine and feel as true *will* and *must* come to pass.

A young woman named Shara G. came to me close to despair. She was involved in a lengthy, complicated lawsuit that had been through one postponement after another, with no end in sight. Her deepest desire was for a harmonious solution to the suit. Her mental imagery, however, was full of failure, loss, bankruptcy, and poverty. The result was just as Coué would have predicted. Her imagination prevailed over her desire, and the suit dragged on and on.

At my suggestion, Shara put herself into a sleepy, drowsy state each night at bedtime, then began to imagine the best possible ending to her problem. She put herself into a state of feeling it to the best of her ability. She knew that the image in her mind had to agree with her heart's desire.

As she became drowsy, she began to imagine as vividly as possible a meeting with her lawyer after the lawsuit was settled. She heard herself asking him questions about the outcome and listening to his explanations. She heard him telling her over and over again, "The case has been settled out of court. This is a perfectly harmonious solution."

During the day, when fear thoughts came into her mind, Shara would run her mental videotape of the meeting with her lawyer, complete with words and gestures. She imagined his smile, his mannerisms, the sound of his voice, the specific words he used. She did this so often, so faithfully, that her fears were counteracted before she even knew they had tried to come into her mind.

At the end of a few weeks, her attorney called her. He confirmed what she had been imagining and feeling as true. The lawsuit was settled, and she knew that the settlement was one she could accept as harmonious.

This is really what the psalmist meant when he wrote:

May all that I say and think [your thoughts and mental images] *be acceptable to thee, O Lord* [the law of your subconscious mind], *my rock and my redeemer!* [the power and wisdom of your subconscious mind that can redeem you from sickness, bondage, and misery]. (Psalm 19:14)

IDEAS TO REMEMBER

1. Mental coercion or too much effort shows anxiety and fear that block your answer. Easy does it.

2. When your mind is relaxed and you accept an idea, your subconscious goes to work to execute the idea.

3. Think and plan independently of traditional methods. Know that there is always an answer and a solution to every problem.

4. Do not be overly concerned with the beating of your heart, with the breathing of your lungs, or the functions of any organ of your body. Lean heavily upon your subconscious and proclaim frequently that divine right action is taking place.

5. The feeling of health produces health, the feeling of wealth produces wealth. How do you feel?

6. Imagination is your most powerful faculty. Imagine what is lovely and of good report. You are what you imagine yourself to be.

7. You avoid conflict between your conscious and subconscious in the sleepy state. Imagine the fulfillment of your desire over and over again prior to sleep. Sleep in peace and wake in joy.

To affirm is to state that it is so, and as you maintain this attitude of mind as true regardless of all evidence to the contrary, you will receive an answer to your prayer.

Chapter Nine

How to Use the Power of Your Subconscious Mind for Wealth

Decide to be wealthy the easy way, with the infallible aid of your subconscious mind. Trying to accumulate wealth by the sweat of your brow and hard labor is one way to become the richest man in the graveyard.

If you are having financial difficulties, if you are trying to make ends meet, it means you have not convinced your subconscious mind that you will always have plenty and some to spare. You know men and women who work a few hours a week and make fabulous sums of money. They do not strive or slave hard. Do not believe the story that the only way you can become wealthy is by the sweat of your brow and hard labor. It is not so; the effortless way of life is the best. Do the thing you love to do, and do it for the joy and thrill of it.

I know an executive in Los Angeles who receives a six-figure salary. Last year he went on a nine-month cruise seeing the world and its beauty spots. He said to me that he had succeeded in convincing his subconscious mind that he is worth that much money. He told me that there are people in his organization earning about one-tenth as much as he does who know more about the business than he does and could probably manage it better. However, they have no ambition and no creative ideas. They are not interested in the wonders of their subconscious mind.

Wealth Is of the Mind

Wealth is ultimately nothing more than a subconscious conviction on the part of the individual. You will not become a millionaire by saying, "I am a millionaire, I am a millionaire." You will grow into a wealth consciousness by building into your mentality the idea of wealth and abundance.

Your Invisible Means of Support

The trouble with most people is that they have no invisible means of support. When business falls away, the stock market drops, or they take a loss on their investments, they seem helpless. The reason for such insecurity is that they do not know how to tap the subconscious mind. They are unacquainted with the inexhaustible storehouse within.

Someone with a poverty-type mind finds himself in poverty-stricken conditions. Someone else, with a mind filled with ideas of wealth, is surrounded by everything he needs. It was never intended that we should lead a life of indigence. You can have wealth, everything you need, and plenty to spare. Your words have power to cleanse your mind of wrong ideas and to instill right ideas in their place.

The Ideal Method for Building Wealth Consciousness

Perhaps you are saying as you read this chapter, "I need wealth and success." This is what you do: Repeat to yourself, for about five minutes three or four times a day, "Wealth. Success." These words have tremendous power. They represent the inner power of the subconscious mind. Anchor your mind on this substantial power within you; then conditions and circumstances corresponding to their nature and quality will be manifested in your life. You are not saying, "I am wealthy," you are dwelling on real powers within you. There is no conflict in the mind when you say, "Wealth." Furthermore, the feeling of wealth will well up within you as you dwell on the idea of wealth.

The feeling of wealth produces wealth; keep this in mind at all times. Your subconscious mind is like a bank, a sort of universal financial institution. It magnifies whatever you deposit or impress upon it whether it is the idea of wealth or of poverty. Choose wealth.

Why Your Affirmations for Wealth Fail

I have talked to many people over the years whose usual complaint is "I have said for weeks and months, 'I am wealthy, I am prosperous,' and nothing has happened." I discovered that when they said, "I am prosperous, I am wealthy," they felt within that they were lying to themselves.

One man told me, "I have affirmed that I am prosperous until I am tired. Things are now worse. I knew when I made the statement that it was obviously not true." His statements were rejected by the conscious mind, and the opposite of what he outwardly affirmed and claimed was made manifest.

Your affirmation succeeds best when it is specific and when it does not produce a mental conflict or argument. The statements made by this man made matters worse because they suggested his lack. Your subconscious accepts what you really feel to be true, not just idle words or statements. The dominant idea or belief is always accepted by the subconscious mind.

How to Avoid Mental Conflict

The following is the ideal way to overcome this conflict for those who have this difficulty. Make this practical statement frequently, particularly prior to sleep: "By day and by night I am being prospered in all of my interests." This affirmation will not arouse any argument because it does not contradict your subconscious mind's impression of financial lack.

I suggested to one businessman whose sales and finances were extremely low and who was greatly worried that he sit down in his office, become quiet, and repeat this statement over and over: "My sales are improving every day." This statement engaged the cooperation of the conscious and subconscious mind, and results followed.

Don't Sign Blank Checks

You sign blank checks when you make such statements as "There is not enough to go around," "There is a shortage," "I will lose the house because I can't meet the mortgage," and so forth. If you are full of fear about the future, you are also writing a blank check and attracting negative conditions to you. Your subconscious mind accepts your fear and negative statement as your request and proceeds in its own way to bring obstacles, delays, lack, and limitation into your life.

Wealth is a subconscious conviction. Build into your mentality the idea of wealth.

Your true source of wealth consists of the ideas in your mind. You can have an idea worth millions of dollars. Your subconscious will give you the idea you seek.

The block to wealth is in your own mind. Destroy that block by getting on good mental terms with everyone.

Your Subconscious Mind Gives You Compound Interest

To him that hath the feeling of wealth, more wealth shall be added; to him that hath the feeling of lack, more lack shall be added. Your subconscious multiplies and magnifies whatever you deposit in it. Every morning as you awaken, deposit thoughts of prosperity, success, wealth, and peace. Dwell upon these concepts. Busy your mind with them as often as possible. These constructive thoughts will find their way as deposits in your subconscious mind, and bring forth abundance and prosperity.

Why Nothing Happened

I can hear you saying, "Oh, I did that, and nothing happened." You did not get results because you indulged in fear thoughts perhaps ten minutes later and neutralized the good you had affirmed. When you place a seed in the ground, you do not dig it up again later in the day. You let it take root and grow.

Suppose, for example, you are about to say, "I will not be able to make that payment." Before you get further than "I will—" stop the sentence. Change it into a constructive statement, such as, "I will be prospered in all my ways."

True Source of Wealth

Your subconscious mind is never short of ideas. There are within it an infinite number of ideas ready to flow into your conscious mind and appear as cash in your pocket in countless ways. This process will continue to go on in your mind regardless of whether the stock market goes up or down, or whether the euro or the dollar drops in value. Your wealth is never truly dependent on bonds, stocks, or money in the bank; these are only symbols—necessary and useful, of course, but only symbols.

The point I want to emphasize is that if you convince your subconscious mind that wealth is yours and that it is always circulating in your life, you will always and inevitably have it, regardless of the form it takes.

Trying to Make Ends Meet and the Real Cause of Lack

There are many people who claim that they are always trying to make ends meet. They seem to have a great struggle to meet their obligations. Have you listened to their conversation? In many instances their conversation runs along this vein. They are constantly condemning those who have succeeded in life and who have raised their heads above the crowd. Perhaps they are saying, "Oh, that fellow has a racket; he is ruthless: he is a crook."

This is why they lack. They are constantly condemning the thing they claim to desire and want. The reason they speak critically of their more prosperous associates is because they are envious and covetous of the other's prosperity. The quickest way to cause wealth to take wings and fly away is to criticize and condemn others who have more wealth than you.

A Common Stumbling Block to Wealth

There is one emotion that is the cause of the lack of wealth in the lives of many. Most people learn this the hard way. It is *envy*. For example, if you see a competitor depositing large sums of money in the bank and you have only a meager amount to deposit, does it make you envious? The way to overcome this emotion is to say to yourself, "Isn't it wonderful! I rejoice in that man's prosperity. I wish for him greater and greater wealth."

To entertain envious thoughts is devastating, because it places you in a negative position. Therefore, wealth flows away from you instead of to you. If you are ever annoyed or irritated by the prosperity or great wealth of another, claim immediately that you truly wish for him or her greater wealth in every possible way. This will neutralize the negative thoughts in your mind and cause an ever-greater measure of wealth to flow to you by the law of your own subconscious mind.

Rubbing Out a Great Mental Block to Wealth

If you are worried and critical about someone who you claim is making money dishonestly, stop worrying about him. If your suspicions are correct, you know that such a person is using the law of mind negatively. In time, the law of mind will take care of him. Be careful not to criticize him, for the reasons previously indicated. Remember: The block or obstacle to wealth is in your own mind. You can now destroy that mental block. This you may do by getting on good mental terms with everyone.

Sleep and Grow Rich

As you go to sleep at night, practice the following technique. Repeat the word *wealth* quietly, easily, and with feeling. Do this over and over again, just like a lullaby. Lull yourself to sleep with the one word, *wealth*. You should be amazed at the result. Wealth should flow to you in avalanches of abundance. This is another example of the magic power of your subconscious mind.

IDEAS TO REMEMBER

1. Decide to be wealthy the easy way, with the infallible aid of your subconscious mind.

2. Trying to accumulate wealth by the sweat of your brow and hard labor is one way to become the richest man in the graveyard. You do not have to strive or slave hard.

3. Wealth is a subconscious conviction. Build into your mentality the idea of wealth.

4. The trouble with most people is that they have no invisible means of support.

5. Repeat the word *wealth* to yourself slowly and quietly for about five minutes prior to sleep and your subconscious will bring wealth to pass in your experience.

6. The feeling of wealth produces wealth. Keep this in mind at all times.

7. Your conscious and subconscious minds must agree. Your subconscious accepts what you feel to be true. The dominant idea is always accepted by your subconscious mind. The dominant idea should be wealth, not poverty.

8. You can overcome any mental conflict regarding wealth by affirming frequently, "By day and by night I am being prospered in all of my interests."

9. Increase your sales by repeating this statement over and over, "My sales are improving every day; I am advancing, progressing, and getting wealthier every day."

10. Stop writing blank checks, such as, "There is not enough to go around" or "There is a shortage," and so forth. Such statements magnify and multiply your loss.

11. Deposit thoughts of prosperity, wealth, and success in your subconscious mind and the latter will give you compound interest.

12. What you consciously affirm, you must not mentally deny a few moments later. This will neutralize the good you have affirmed.

13. Your true source of wealth consists of the ideas in your mind. You can have an idea worth millions of dollars. Your subconscious will give you the idea you seek.

14. Envy and jealousy are stumbling blocks to the flow of wealth. Rejoice in the prosperity of others.

15. The block to wealth is in your own mind. Destroy that block now by getting on good mental terms with everyone.

Don't make money your sole aim. Claim wealth, happiness, peace, true expression, and love, and personally radiate love and goodwill to all. Then your subconscious mind will give you compound interest in all these fields of expression.

Chapter Ten

Your Right to Be Rich

Your conscious and subconscious mind must agree. Your subconscious accepts what you really feel to be true. This dominant idea is always accepted by your subconscious mind. The dominant idea should be wealth not poverty.

You have a fundamental right to be rich. You are here to lead the abundant life and be happy, radiant, and free. You should, therefore, have all the money you need to lead a full, happy, and prosperous life.

You are here to grow, expand, and unfold spiritually, mentally, and materially. You have the inalienable right to fully develop and express yourself in all your potentials. An important aspect of that is the ability, should you so choose, to surround yourself with beauty and luxury.

Why be satisfied with just enough to go around when you can enjoy the riches of your subconscious mind? In this chapter, you will learn to make friends with money. Once you do, you will always have all you need and more. Don't let anyone make you feel doubtful or ashamed of your desire to be rich. At its deepest level, it is a desire for a fuller, happier, more wonderful life. It is a cosmic urge. It is not only good but very good.

Money Is a Symbol

Money is a symbol of exchange. To you it is a symbol not only of freedom from want but also of beauty, refinement, abundance, and luxury. It is also a symbol of the economic health of the nation. When your blood is circulating freely in your body, you are healthy. When money is circulating freely in your life, you are economically healthy. When people begin to hoard money, to put it away in tin boxes and become charged with fear, they become economically ill.

As a symbol, money has taken many forms throughout the centuries. Almost anything you can think of has served as money at some time and place in history—gold and silver, of course, but also salt, beads, and trinkets of various kinds. In early times people's wealth was often determined by the number of sheep and oxen they owned. Now we use currency and other negotiable instruments. One reason is obvious. It is much more convenient to write a check than to carry a few sheep around with you to pay bills.

How to Walk the Royal Road to Riches

Once you understand the powers of your subconscious mind, you have within your grasp a road map to the royal road to riches of all kinds—spiritual, mental, or financial. Anyone who has taken the trouble to learn the laws of mind believes and knows definitively that she will never want. Regardless of economic crises, stock-market fluctuations, recessions, strikes, galloping inflation, or even war, she will always be amply supplied.

The reason for this is that she has conveyed the idea of wealth to her subconscious mind. As a result, it keeps her supplied wherever she may be. She has convinced herself in her mind that money is forever flowing freely in her life and that there is always a wonderful surplus available to her. As she decrees it, so it is. Should there be a financial collapse tomorrow and everything she possesses becomes worthless, she will still attract wealth. She will come through the crisis comfortably and likely even gain advantage from it.

Why You Do Not Have More Money

As you read this chapter, you may be thinking, "I deserve a bigger income than I have." In my opinion, that is true of most people. They really do deserve to have more—but they are not likely to get it. One of the most important reasons these people do not have more money is that they silently or openly condemn it. They refer to money as "filthy lucre." They tell their children and friends that "the love of money is the root of all evil." Coupled with this as a reason they do not prosper is that they have a sneaky subconscious feeling there is some special virtue in poverty. This subconscious pattern may be due to early-childhood training, or it may be based on a false interpretation of scriptures.

Money and a Balanced Life

One time a man came up to me and said, "I am broke. But that's all right. I do not like money. It is the root of all evil." These statements represent the thinking of a confused, neurotic mind. Love of money to the exclusion of everything else will cause you to become lopsided and unbalanced. You are here to use your power or authority wisely. Some people crave power, others crave money.

If you set your heart on money exclusively and say, "Money

is all I want; I am going to give all my attention to amassing money; nothing else matters," you can get money and gain a fortune, but at what cost! You have forgotten that you are here to lead a balanced life. You must also satisfy the hunger for peace of mind, harmony, love, joy, and perfect health.

By making money your sole aim, you made a wrong choice. You thought that was all you wanted, but you found after all your efforts that it was not only the money you needed. No one on his deathbed wishes he had spent more time making money! You also desire true expression of your hidden talents, true place in life, beauty, and the joy of contributing to the welfare and success of others. By learning the laws of your subconscious mind, you could have a million dollars or many millions, if you wanted them, and still have peace of mind, harmony, perfect health, and perfect expression.

Poverty Is a Mental Illness

There is no virtue in poverty. It is an illness like any other mental illness. If you were physically ill, you would realize there was something wrong with you. You would seek help and try to cure the condition at once. In the same way, if you do not have enough money constantly circulating in your life, there is something radically wrong with you.

The urge of the life-principle in you is toward growth, expansion, and the life more abundant. You are not here to live in a hovel, dress in rags, and go hungry. You should be happy, prosperous, and successful.

Why You Must Never Criticize Money

Cleanse your mind of all weird and superstitious beliefs about money. Do not ever regard money as evil or filthy. If you do, you cause it to take wings and fly away from you.

Remember that you lose what you condemn. You cannot attract what you criticize.

Getting the Right Attitude Toward Money

Here is a simple technique you may use to multiply money in your experience. Use the following statements several times a day:

> I like money. I love it. I use it wisely, constructively, and judiciously. Money is constantly circulating in my life. I release it with joy, and it returns to me multiplied in a wonderful way. It is good and very good. Money flows to me in avalanches of abundance. I use it for good only, and I am grateful for my good and for the riches of my mind.

How the Scientific Thinker Looks at Money

Suppose you discovered a rich vein of gold, silver, lead, copper, or iron in the ground. Would you announce that these things are evil? Of course not! All evil comes from humankind's darkened understanding, from ignorance, from false interpretation of life, and from misuse of the subconscious mind.

Since money is simply a symbol, we could just as easily use lead or tin or some other metal as a medium of exchange. In the earlier part of the twentieth century, U.S. dimes and quarters were made of silver. At times, they contained ten cents' or twenty-five cents' worth of silver. Then the government started making them of cheaper metals. But the worth of a quarter is still twenty-five cents, even if the metal that makes it up is worth far less than that.

A physicist will tell you that the only difference between one metal and another is the kind and number of elementary particles in its atoms. If you direct a stream of particles at a block of one metal, you can change it into another. The alchemist's ancient dream of producing gold from baser metals is now within our grasp. But so what? Gold is no more virtuous, or evil, than lead. They are different substances with different properties, that's all. It is only because of the long history in which gold was considered especially precious that people love it—or hate it—more than they do lead.

> *You can overcome any mental conflict regarding wealth by affirming frequently, "By day and by night I am being prospered in all of my interests."*

> *Envy and jealousy are stumbling blocks to the flow of wealth. Rejoice in the prosperity of others.*

> *Never use the term "filthy rich" or say "I despise money." You lose what you criticize. There is nothing good or bad about money but thinking of it in either light makes it so.*

How to Attract the Money You Need

Many years ago I met a young man in Australia who told me that his fondest dream was to become a physician. He was taking science classes and doing brilliantly, but he had no way to pay for medical school. His parents were both dead. To support himself, he cleaned doctors' offices in the local hospital's professional building. I explained to him that a seed planted in the soil attracts to itself everything it needs for its proper unfolding. All he had to do was to take a lesson from the seed and plant the required idea in his subconscious mind.

Every night, as this young man went to sleep, he visualized a medical diploma with his name in big, bold letters. He found it easy to create a sharp, detailed image of the diploma. Part of his job was to dust and polish the framed diplomas hanging on the walls of the doctors' offices, and he studied them as he cleaned them.

He persisted with this visualization technique every night for about four months. Then one of the doctors whose office he cleaned asked if he would like to become a physician's assistant. The doctor paid for him to attend a training program where he learned a wide variety of medical skills, then gave him a job as his assistant. He was so impressed with the young man's brilliance and determination that he later helped him through medical school. Today, this young man is a prominent doctor in Montreal, Canada.

This young man's success came because he had learned the law of attraction. He discovered how to use his subconscious mind the right way. This involved making use of an age-old law that says, "Having clearly seen the end, you have willed the means to the realization of the end." The end in this case was to become a physician. He was able to imagine, see, and feel the reality of being a doctor. He lived with the idea. He sustained it, nourished it, and loved it. At last, through his visualization, the idea penetrated the layers of his subconscious mind. It became a conviction. That conviction then attracted to him everything that was needed for the fulfillment of his dream.

Why Some People Do Not Get a Raise in Pay

Let us say you work for a large corporation. You believe that you are underpaid. You resent the fact that you are not appreciated by your employers. You constantly mull over your conviction that you deserve more money and greater recognition.

By setting yourself in mental opposition to your employer,

you are subconsciously severing your ties with that organization. You are setting a process in motion. Then, one day, your superior tells you, "We have to let you go." In a real sense, you dismissed yourself. Your superior was simply acting as the instrument through which your own negative mental state was confirmed. This is an example of the law of action and reaction. The action is your thought, and the reaction is the response of your subconscious mind.

Obstacles and Impediments
on the Pathway to Riches

From time to time, you have probably heard someone say, "Anybody who makes a lot of money has to be some kind of crook."

The person who talks—and thinks—this way is usually suffering from a financial illness. Maybe he is bitter and envious of former friends who have been more successful and now have greater resources. If so, this person is creating his own difficulties. Entertaining negative thoughts about those friends and condemning their wealth causes prosperity and wealth to flee. Would you stay with someone who condemns you? Of course not; and neither will wealth. This person is chasing away the thing he is praying for.

He is praying in two ways. On the one hand he is saying, "I wish wealth to flow to me now." But in the next breath, he is saying, "That fellow's wealth is a dirty, evil thing." This contradiction is a signpost on the road to poverty and misery. Always make it a special point to rejoice in the wealth of another person.

Protect Your Investments

If you are seeking guidance regarding investments, or if you are worried about your stocks or bonds, quietly claim, "Infinite Intelligence governs and watches over all my financial transactions. Whatsoever I do shall prosper." If you do this frequently, with perfect faith and confidence, you will find that you will be guided to make wise investments. Moreover, you will be protected from loss, because you will be prompted to sell any risky securities or holdings before any loss accrues to you.

You Cannot Get Something for Nothing

In large stores the management hires guards and store detectives to keep people from stealing. Every day they catch a number of people trying to get something for nothing. Anyone who does such a thing is steeped in a mental atmosphere of lack and limitation. In trying to steal from others, they are robbing themselves of peace, harmony, faith, honesty, integrity, goodwill, and confidence.

Furthermore, their messages to their subconscious minds draw to them all manner of loss: loss of character, prestige, social status, and peace of mind. These people do not understand how their minds work. They lack faith in the source of supply. If only they would mentally call on the powers of their subconscious mind and claim that they are guided to their true expression, they would find work and abundance. Then, by honesty, integrity, and perseverance, they would become a credit to themselves and to society at large.

Your Constant Supply of Money

The path to freedom, comfort, and a constant supply of needed wealth lies in recognizing the powers of your subconscious mind and the creative power of your thought or mental image. Accept the abundant life in your own mind. Your mental acceptance and expectancy of wealth has its own mathematics and mechanics of expression. As you enter into the mood of opulence, all things necessary for the abundant life will come to pass.

Let this be your daily affirmation; write it in your heart:

I am one with the infinite riches of my subconscious mind. It is my right to be rich, happy, and successful. Money flows to me freely, copiously, and endlessly. I am forever conscious of my true worth. I give of my talents freely, and I am wonderfully blessed financially. It is wonderful!

IDEAS TO REMEMBER

1. Be bold enough to claim that it is your right to be rich. Your deeper mind will honor your claim.

2. You don't want just enough to go around. You want all the money you need to do all the things you want to do, when you want to do them. Get acquainted with the riches of your subconscious mind.

3. When money is circulating freely in your life, you are economically healthy. Look at money like the tide and you will always have plenty of it. The ebb and flow of the tide is constant. When the tide is out, you are absolutely sure that it will return.

4. Knowing the laws of your subconscious mind, you will always be supplied regardless of what form money takes.

5. One reason many people simply make ends meet and never have enough money is that they condemn money. What you condemn takes wings and flies away.

6. Do not make a god of money. It is only a symbol. Remember that the real riches are in your mind. You are here to lead a balanced life—this includes acquiring all the money you need.

7. Don't make money your sole aim. Claim wealth, happiness, peace to all. Then your subconscious mind will give you compound interest in all these fields of expression.

8. There is no virtue in poverty. It is a disease of the mind. You should heal yourself of this mental conflict or malady at once.

9. You are not here to live in a hovel, to dress in rags, or to go hungry. You are here to lead the life more abundant.

10. Never use the term "filthy lucre" or say "I despise money." You lose what you criticize. Money in itself is neither good nor bad but thinking of it in either light makes it so.

11. Repeat frequently, "I like money. I use it wisely, constructively, and judiciously. I release it with joy, and it returns a thousandfold."

12. Money is not evil any more than copper, lead, tin, or iron that you may find in the ground. All evil is due to ignorance and misuse of the mind's powers.

13. To picture the end result in your mind causes your subconscious to respond and fulfill your mental picture.

14. Stop trying to get something for nothing. There is no such thing as a free lunch. You must give to receive. If

you give mental attention to your goals, ideals, and enterprises, your deeper mind will back you up. The key to wealth is to apply the laws of the subconscious mind by impregnating it with the idea of wealth.

Do not make a god of money. It is only a symbol. Remember that the real riches are in your mind. You are here to lead a balanced life—this includes acquiring all the money you need.

Chapter Eleven

Your Subconscious Mind as a Partner in Success

The true inner meaning of success is to be successful at the enterprise of living. A long period of peace, joy, and happiness on this plane may be termed success. The eternal experience of these qualities is the everlasting life spoken of by Jesus. The real things of life, such as peace, harmony, integrity, security, and happiness, are intangible. They come from the deep self of human beings. Meditating on these qualities builds these treasures of heaven in our subconscious. That is the true place where

> *. . . there is no moth and no rust to spoil it, no thieves to break in and steal.* (Matthew 6:20)

The Three Steps to Success

The vital first step to success is to find out the thing you love to do, then do it. Unless you love your work, you cannot possibly consider yourself successful at it, even if all the rest of the world hails you as a great success. Loving your work, you have a deep desire to carry it out. If someone is drawn to become a psychiatrist, it is not enough for her to get a diploma and hang it on the wall. She will want to keep up with the field, attend conventions, and continue studying the mind and its workings. She will visit other clinics and pore over the latest scientific journals. In other words, she will work to keep herself informed in the most advanced methods of alleviating human suffering, because she puts the interests of her patients first.

But what if, as you read these words, you find yourself thinking, "I can't take the first step, because I don't know what it is I want to do. How on earth do I find a field of effort that I will love?"

If that is your situation, pray for guidance in this way: The Infinite Intelligence of my subconscious mind reveals to me my true place in life.

Repeat this prayer quietly, positively, and lovingly to your deeper mind. As you persist with faith and confidence, the answer will come to you as a feeling, a hunch, or a tendency in a certain direction. It will come to you clearly and in peace, and as an inner silent awareness.

The second step to success is to specialize in some particular branch of work and strive to excel in it. Suppose a student chooses chemistry as a profession. He should concentrate on one of the many branches in this field and give all his time and attention to his chosen specialty. His enthusiasm should make him want to know all there is available about his field; if possible, he should know more than anyone else. The young man should become ardently interested in his work and should desire to use it to serve the world.

He that is greatest among you, let him become your servant. There is an enormous contrast between this attitude of mind and that of someone who wants only to make a living or just "get by." "Getting by" is not true success. People's motives must be greater, nobler, and more altruistic. They must serve others, thereby casting their bread upon the waters.

The third step is the most important one. You must be sure that the thing you want to do does not contribute only to your own success. Your desire must not be selfish. It must benefit humanity. The path of a complete circuit must be formed. In other words, your idea must go forth with the purpose of blessing or serving the world. It will then come back to you magnified and full of blessings. If you work only for your own benefit, you do not complete this essential circuit. You may appear to be successful, but the short-circuit you have generated in your life may lead over time to limitation or sickness.

The Measure of True Success

At this point you may be thinking, "What about that guy I saw a show about? The one who made hundreds of millions of dollars from shady stock deals? He's as big a success as you'll ever see, and I don't think he cares a bit about benefiting humanity."

Such cases are all too common, but we must be careful to understand them for what they are. Someone may seem to succeed for a while, but money obtained by fraud often takes wings and flies away. Even if it does not, when we rob from another, we rob from ourselves. The mood of lack and limitation that led to our behavior manifests itself in other ways as well, in our body, our home life, our relationships with others.

What we think and feel, we create. We create what we believe. Even though someone may have accumulated a fortune fraudulently, he is not successful. There is no success without peace of mind. What good is a person's accumulated wealth if he cannot sleep nights, is sick, or has a guilt complex?

I once met a professional criminal in London who told me something of his exploits. He had amassed a large fortune that allowed him to live in luxury in his house outside London and his summer home in France. In luxury, yes, but *not* in comfort. He was in constant dread of being arrested by Scotland Yard. He had many inner disorders that were undoubtedly caused by his constant fear and deep-seated guilt complex. He knew he had done wrong. This deep sense of guilt attracted all kinds of trouble to him.

Later, I heard that he had voluntarily turned himself in to the police and had served a prison sentence. After his release from prison, he sought psychological and spiritual counsel and became transformed. He went to work and became an honest, law-abiding citizen. He found what he loved to do and was happy.

A successful person loves her work and expresses herself fully. Success is contingent upon a higher ideal than the mere accumulation of riches. The person of success is the person who possesses great psychological and spiritual understanding. Many of the great business leaders of today depend upon the correct use of their subconscious minds for their success. They cultivate the ability to see an upcoming project as if it were already complete. Having seen and felt the fulfillment of their prayers, their subconscious minds bring about their realization. If you imagine an objective dearly, you will be provided with the necessities, in ways you know not of, through the wonder-working power of your subconscious mind.

In considering the three steps to success you must never forget the underlying power of the creative forces of your subconscious mind. This is the energy behind all the steps in any plan of success. Your thought is creative. Thought fused with feeling becomes a subjective faith or belief—

As you have believed, so let it be. (Matthew 9:29)

Once you understand that you possess a mighty force within you that is capable of bringing to pass all your desires, you gain both confidence and a sense of peace. Whatever your field of action may be, you should learn the laws of your subconscious mind. When you know how to apply the powers of your mind and when you are expressing yourself fully and giving of your talents to others, you are on the sure path to true success. If you are about God's business, or any part of it, God, by his nature, is for you, so who can be against you? With this understanding there is no power in heaven or on earth that can withhold success from you.

How He Made His Dream Come True

In Hollywood, I met an actor whose name is probably familiar to every moviegoer or television fan. He confided to me that he had grown up on a small farm in the Midwest. His family was just scraping by. His only entertainment was an old black-and-white TV that barely pulled in two channels. Even so, he began to dream of being an actor. The dream occupied him more and more.

"All the time I was out working in the fields," he said, "or driving the cows back to the barn, I imagined that I could see my name in big letters on the marquee of a great theater. I saw every detail—the crowds of fans, the interviewers clamoring to speak to me. I kept this up for years.

"Finally, I left home. I came to Los Angeles and got work as an extra in films and TV shows. Before long, I got my first starring role. The night of the premiere, I drove to the theater and almost fainted. There was my name in lights, there were the crowds and the news reporters, all just as I had imagined them as a child. I, more than anyone, understand how the power of sustained imagination can bring success."

Her Dream Pharmacy Became a Reality

Some years ago I got to know a young pharmacist named Mary S. She worked in the prescription department of a big chain drugstore. One day while she was filling a prescription for me, we started talking. I asked her how she liked her work.

"Oh, it's fine," she said. "Between my salary and commissions, I do okay, and the company has a good profit-sharing program. With any luck, I'll be able to retire while I'm still young enough to enjoy life."

I was silent for a moment. Then I asked, "Was that the way you thought it would be as a child, when you decided you wanted to be a pharmacist?"

Her face grew troubled. "Well, no," she replied. "I guess not. I always saw myself with my own store. I wanted to walk down the street and have people say hello to me and call me by name. And I'd know all their names, because I was their druggist. You're going to think this is strange, but I even dreamed about having parents call me in the middle of the night because their kid was sick. I'd pull my clothes on over my pajamas and go down to the store to get them the medicine they needed. Not much like a nine-to-five job behind a counter at the back end of a big store, is it?"

"It certainly isn't," I said. "But why shouldn't you follow your dream? Wouldn't you be happier and more productive? Raise your sights. Get out of this place. Start your own store."

"How can I?" she said, shaking her head. "That takes big money, and we're just getting by from month to month."

My response was to share with her a wonderful fact: Whatever she could conceive as true, she could bring into being. I went on to tell her something about the powers of her subconscious mind. She soon understood that if she could succeed in impregnating her subconscious mind with a clear and specific idea, those powers would somehow bring it to pass.

She began to imagine that she was in her own store. She mentally arranged the bottles, dispensed prescriptions, and imagined waiting on customers who were also her neighbors and friends. She also visualized a big bank balance. Mentally she worked in that imaginary store. Like a good actor, she lived the role. *Act as though I am, and I will be.* She put herself wholeheartedly into the act, living, moving, and acting on the assumption that she owned the store.

Several years later, Mary wrote me to say what had happened to her life since our conversation. The chain store she worked for went under because of competition from a larger store at a new mall. She found a job as a traveling representative for a major drug company, handling a territory that covered several states.

One day her work took her to a small town on the western edge of her territory. There was only one drugstore in town. She had never been there before, but the moment she walked in, she recognized it. It was exactly the store she had visualized so clearly in her imagination.

Flabbergasted, she told the elderly owner of the drugstore

about this amazing coincidence. In turn, the owner confided that he was about ready to retire but did not want to sell a store that had been in his family for three generations to some big corporation.

After several discussions, the owner offered to lend her the money to buy the store. She would be able to make the payments on the loan out of the profits of the business. The young woman moved her family to the town and soon was able to make a down payment on a big old house within walking distance of the store. Now, when she walks to work in the morning, everyone she passes says hello and calls her by name. They know her, because she is their druggist.

Remember that the thankful heart is always close to the riches of the universe.

Increase your sales by repeating this statement over and over again: "My sales are improving every day; I am advancing, progressing, and getting wealthier every day."

Stop writing blank checks, such as "There is not enough to go around" or "There is a shortage." Such statements magnify and multiply your loss.

Using the Subconscious Mind in Business

Some years ago I gave a lecture to a group of business executives on the powers of imagination and the subconscious mind. In the course of the lecture, I described how the great German poet Goethe used his imagination wisely when confronted with difficulties and predicaments.

According to Goethe's biographers, he was accustomed to filling many hours quietly holding imaginary conversations. He would imagine one of his friends sitting across from him, answering him in the right way. In other words, if he were concerned over any problems, he imagined his friend giving him the right or appropriate answer, accompanied with his usual gestures and tonal qualities of the voice. He made the entire imaginary scene as real and as vivid as possible.

One of the people present at this lecture was a young stockbroker. She proceeded to adopt the technique of Goethe. She began to have imaginary conversations with a multimillionaire investor who knew her and had once congratulated her on her wise and sound judgment in recommending stocks. She dramatized this imaginary conversation until she had psychologically fixed it as a form of belief in her mind.

This broker's inner talking and controlled imagination certainly agreed with her aim, which was to make sound investments for her clients. Her main purpose in life was to make money for her clients and to see them prosper financially by her wise counsel. She is still using her subconscious mind in her business, and she is a brilliant success in her field. She was recently interviewed in an article in a major financial magazine.

A Boy Turns Failure into Success

Sixteen-year-old Todd M. told me, "I'm failing everything. I don't know why. I guess I'm just stupid. Maybe I'd better drop out of school before they flunk me out."

As we talked further, I discovered that the only thing wrong with Todd was his attitude. He felt indifferent toward his studies and resentful toward some of his teachers and fellow students.

I taught him how to use his subconscious mind to succeed in his studies. He began to affirm certain truths several times a day, particularly at night just prior to sleep and first thing after awakening in the morning. As we have seen, these are the best times to impregnate the subconscious mind.

He affirmed as follows:

I realize that my subconscious mind is a storehouse of memory. It retains everything I read and hear from my teachers. I have a perfect memory at my disposal, if I choose to use it. The Infinite Intelligence of my subconscious mind constantly reveals to me everything I need to know on all my examinations, whether written or oral. I radiate love and goodwill to all my teachers and fellow students. I sincerely wish for them success and all good things.

Todd is now enjoying a greater freedom than he has ever known. He is now receiving all A's. He constantly imagines the teachers and his parents congratulating him on his success in his studies.

How to Become Successful in Buying and Selling

In buying or selling, remember that your conscious mind is the starter and your subconscious mind is the motor. You must start the motor to enable it to perform its work. Your conscious mind awakens the power of your subconscious mind.

The first step in conveying your clarified desire, idea, or image to the deeper mind is to relax, immobilize the attention, get still, and be quiet. This quiet, relaxed, and peaceful attitude of mind prevents extraneous matter and false ideas from interfering with your mental absorption of your ideal. Furthermore, in the quiet, passive, and receptive attitude of mind, effort is reduced to a minimum.

The second step is to begin to imagine the reality of the end you desire. For example, you may wish to buy a home. In your relaxed state of mind, you affirm as follows:

The Infinite Intelligence of my subconscious mind is all-wise. It reveals to me now the ideal home that meets all my requirements and that I can afford. I am now turning this request over to my subconscious mind. I know it responds according to the nature of my request. I release this request with absolute faith and confidence in the same way that a farmer deposits a seed in the ground, trusting implicitly in the laws of growth.

The answer to your prayer may come from an advertisement in the paper or from a friend. Or you may be guided directly to a particular home that is exactly what you are seeking. There are many ways in which your prayer may be answered. The principal knowledge, in which you may place your confidence, is that the answer always comes, provided you trust the working of your deeper mind.

Suppose, instead of wanting to buy, you want to sell a home, land, or any kind of property. The same approach of trusting the Infinite Intelligence of your subconscious mind will give you the guidance you seek. When I sold my own home in Los Angeles, I used a technique that many real-estate brokers I have spoken to are now using with remarkable and speedy results.

I placed a sign on the lawn in front of my home that read "For Sale By Owner." That night, as I was going to sleep, I asked myself, "Suppose you find a buyer for the house, what will you do next?" The answer was "I'll take down the 'For Sale' sign and throw it in the garbage."

Against the inner screen of my mind, I projected a detailed scenario. I took hold of the sign, pulled it up from the ground, placed it on my shoulder, and carried it to the trash cans at the back of the house. As I threw it in the garbage, I said, "Thanks for your help, but I don't need you anymore!"

I went to sleep feeling the deep inner satisfaction of knowing that it was finished.

The next day a man gave me a deposit on the house and said, "You can throw that sign away. You don't need it anymore."

I followed his advice. I pulled the sign up and took it to the garbage. The outer action conformed to the inner. There is nothing new about this. *As within, so without.* In other words, according to the image impressed on your subconscious mind, so it is on the objective screen of your life. The outside mirrors the inside. External action follows internal action.

Here is another effective method used in selling homes, land, or any kind of property. Affirm slowly, quietly, and feelingly as follows:

> Infinite Intelligence attracts to me the buyer for this home who wants it and who prospers in it. This buyer is being sent to me by the creative intelligence of my subconscious mind, which makes no mistakes. This buyer may look at many other homes, but mine is the only one he wants and will buy because he is guided by the Infinite Intelligence within him. I know the buyer is right, the time is right, and the price is right. Everything about it is right. The deeper currents of my subconscious mind are now in operation bringing both of us together in divine order. I know that it is so.

Remember always that what you are seeking is also seeking you. Whenever you want to sell a home or property of any kind, there is always someone who wants what you have to offer. By using the powers of your subconscious mind correctly, you free your mind of all sense of competition and anxiety in buying and selling.

How She Succeeded in Getting What She Wanted

A young woman, Margaret T., regularly attended my lectures and classes. Because of where she lived, she had to change buses three times to get to the hall. It took her one and a half hours each way to attend a lecture. In one of my lectures, she heard me explain how a young man who needed a car in his work received one.

She went home and experimented with the technique I had outlined in my lecture. She later wrote me a letter telling me how she had applied my methods and what followed. I publish it here with her permission.

Dear Dr. Murphy:

I knew that I had to have a car for my personal growth. There was no other way I could go on attending your lectures regularly. I decided that, as long as I was trying to obtain a car, I should try to obtain the car I had always dreamed about, which is a Cadillac.

In my imagination I went through all the steps I would go through if I were actually buying and driving a car. I saw myself going into the showroom and test-driving the model I was interested in. I claimed that Cadillac as my own over and over again.

I kept the mental picture of getting into the car, driving it, feeling the upholstery, and so on, consistently for over two weeks. Last week I drove to your lecture in a Cadillac. My uncle in Inglewood had passed away and left me his Cadillac and his entire estate.

An Executive Success Technique

Many prominent business executives quietly use the abstract term "success" over and over many times a day until they reach a conviction that success is theirs. They know that the idea of success contains all the essential elements of success. Likewise, you can begin now to repeat the word "success" to yourself with faith and conviction. Your subconscious mind will accept it as true of you, and you will be under a subconscious compulsion to succeed.

You are compelled to express your subjective beliefs, impressions, and convictions. What does *success* imply to you? You want, undoubtedly, to be successful in your home life and in your relationships with others. You wish to be outstanding in your chosen work or profession. You wish to possess a beautiful home, and all the money you need to live comfortably and happily. You want to be successful in your spiritual life and in your contact with the powers of your subconscious mind.

You are a business executive also because you are in the business of living. Become a successful executive by imagining yourself doing what you long to do and possessing the things you long to possess. Become imaginative; mentally participate in the reality of the successful state. Make a habit of it. Go to sleep feeling successful every night and perfectly satisfied, and you will eventually succeed in implanting the idea of success in your subconscious mind. Believe you were born to succeed, and wonders will happen as you pray.

IDEAS TO REMEMBER

1. Success means successful living. When you are peaceful, happy, joyous, and doing what you love to do, you are successful.

2. Find out what you love to do, then do it. If you don't know your true expression, ask for guidance, and the lead will come.

3. Specialize in your particular field and try to know more about it than anyone else.

4. Those who are successful are not selfish. Their main desire in life is to serve humanity.

5. There is no true success without peace of mind.

6. A successful person possesses great psychological and spiritual understanding.

7. If you imagine an objective clearly, you will be provided with the necessities through the wonder-working power of your subconscious mind.

8. Your thought fused with feeling becomes a subjective belief, and according to your belief is it done unto you.

9. The power of sustained imagination draws forth the miracle-working powers of your subconscious mind.

10. If you are seeking promotion in your work, imagine your employer, supervisor, or loved one congratulating you on your promotion. Make the picture vivid and real. Hear the voice, see the gestures, and feel the reality of it all. Continue to do this frequently, and through frequent occupancy of your mind, you will experience the joy of the answered prayer.

11. Your subconscious mind is a storehouse of memory. For a perfect memory, affirm frequently: "The Infinite Intelligence of my subconscious mind reveals to me everything I need to know at all times, everywhere."

12. If you wish to sell a home or property of any kind, affirm slowly, quietly, and feelingly as follows: "Infinite Intelligence attracts to me the buyer for this house or property who wants it and who prospers in it." Sustain

this awareness, and the deeper currents of your subconscious mind will bring it to pass.

13. The idea of success contains all the elements of success. Repeat the word *success* to yourself frequently with faith and conviction and you will be under a subconscious compulsion to succeed.

One reason many people simply make ends meet and never have enough money is that they condemn money. What you condemn takes wings and flies away.

Chapter Twelve

How Scientists Use the Subconscious Mind

Experiment scientifically until you prove to yourself that there is always a direct response from the Infinite Intelligence of your subconscious mind to your conscious thinking.

Many of the most creative scientists in history have realized the true importance of the subconscious mind. Edison, Marconi, Einstein, and many others have used the subconscious mind to give them the insight and the "know-how" to bring about their great achievements. The ability to bring into action the power of the subconscious mind is one of the most important factors in determining the success of great scientific and research workers.

One of the most amazing examples of this can be found in the life of the celebrated chemist Friedrich von Stradonitz. He had been struggling for a long time to understand the chemical structure of the hydrocarbon called benzene. This is a compound that contains six atoms of carbon and six of hydrogen. Stradonitz was constantly perplexed by the problem. All his efforts seemed to lead nowhere.

Unable to solve the riddle, tired and exhausted, Stradonitz turned the matter over completely to his subconscious mind. Shortly afterward, as he was about to board a London bus, his subconscious presented his conscious mind with a sudden flash. In his mind, Stradonitz saw the image of a snake biting its own tail and turning around like a pinwheel. This message from his subconscious mind inspired him to orient his search in a different direction. Soon he arrived at the long-sought answer, the circular arrangement of atoms that is known as the benzene ring.

How a Distinguished Scientist Brought Forth His Own Inventions

Nikola Tesla was a brilliant pioneer in the field of electricity. The Tesla coil, an exhibit in science museums that is always a favorite with children, was only one of his inventions. This is a charged metal sphere. When someone touches it, the static electricity makes his or her hair stand straight up. Tesla also experimented with the concept of broadcasting energy. His ideas on this topic are still considered revolutionary.

Tesla was a convinced user of the power of the subconscious mind. Whenever he had an idea for a new invention or a new research direction, he would build it up in his imagination then turn it over to his subconscious mind. He knew that his subconscious mind would reconstruct and reveal to his conscious mind all the parts needed for its manufacture in concrete form. Through quietly contemplating every possible improvement, he wasted no time on correcting defects. He was able to give the technicians working with him the perfect end product of his mind.

In an interview, he said, "Invariably, my device works as I imagined it should. In twenty years there has not been a single exception."

How a Famous Naturalist Solved His Problem

Professor Louis Agassiz of Harvard University was one of the most distinguished American naturalists of the nineteenth century. He discovered the great powers of his subconscious mind while he slept. The following example comes from a biography of Agassiz, written by his widow:

> For two weeks he had been striving to decipher the somewhat obscure impression of a fossil fish on the stone slab in which it was preserved. Weary and perplexed, he put his work aside at last, and tried to dismiss it from his mind. Shortly after, he awakened, convinced that while he was asleep he had seen his fish with all the missing features perfectly restored. But when he tried to hold and make fast the image it escaped him. Nevertheless, he went early the next morning to the Jardin des Plantes, thinking that on looking anew at the impression he should see something, which would put him on the track of his vision. In vain—the blurred record was as black as ever. The next night he saw the fish again, but with no more satisfactory result. When he awoke it disappeared from his memory as before. Hoping that the same experience might be repeated, on the third night he placed a pencil and paper beside his bed before going to sleep.
>
> Accordingly, toward morning the fish reappeared in his dream, confusedly at first, but at last with such distinctness that he had no longer any doubt as to its zoological characters. Still half dreaming, in perfect darkness, he traced these characters on the sheet of paper at the bedside. In the morning he was surprised to see in his nocturnal sketch features which he thought it impossible the fossil itself should reveal. He hastened to the Jardin des Plantes, and, with his drawing

as a guide, succeeded in chiseling away the surface of the stone under which portions of the fish proved to be hidden. When wholly exposed, it corresponded with his dream and his drawing, and he succeeded in classifying it with ease.

How an Outstanding Physician Solved the Problem of Diabetes

In the 1920s, Dr. Frederick Banting, a brilliant Canadian physician and researcher, focused his attention on the ravages of diabetes. At that time medical science offered no effective method of arresting the disease. Dr. Banting spent considerable time experimenting and studying the international literature on the subject, but every path he explored seemed to be a dead end.

One night, exhausted by still another long day of what seemed to be wasted efforts, he fell asleep. While he lay sleeping, his subconscious mind instructed him to extract the residue from the degenerated pancreatic duct of dogs. This inspiration led him to the discovery of insulin, which has helped countless millions of people since.

You will note that Dr. Banting had been consciously dwelling on the problem for some time, seeking a solution, a way out. His subconscious responded accordingly.

It does not follow that you will always get an answer overnight. The answer may not come for some time. Do not be discouraged. Keep on turning the problem over every night to the subconscious mind prior to sleep, as if you had never done it before.

If you continue to experience a delay in arriving at a solution, maybe you are thinking of the question you are presenting to your subconscious mind as a major one that will take a long time to solve. This would not be surprising. We are usually tempted to believe our problems are difficult. If they weren't, they wouldn't be problems. However, this is a mistake. Your subconscious mind is timeless and spaceless. Go to sleep believing you have the answer *now*. Do not postulate that the answer will have to wait to come in the future. Have an abiding faith in the outcome. Become convinced now as you read this book that there is an answer and a perfect solution for you.

Feel the joy and restfulness in foreseeing the certain accomplishment of your desire. Any mental picture which you have in your mind is the substance of things hoped for and the evidence of things not seen.

Scientists meditating on ancient scrolls, temples, fossils, and so on are able to reconstruct scenes of the past and make them alive today. Their subconscious mind comes to their aid.

When you are perplexed, confused, and fearful, and wonder what decision to make, remember that you have an inner guide that will lead and direct you in all your ways, revealing to you the perfect plan and showing you the way you should go.

How a Scientist Escaped from a Soviet Concentration Camp

Dr. Lothar von Blenk-Schmidt, an outstanding electronics engineer, was locked up in a Soviet prison camp during World War II. He credits his survival and eventual escape to freedom to the powers of his subconscious mind.

I was a prisoner of war in a coal mine in Russia, and I saw men dying all around me in that prison compound. We were watched over by brutal guards, arrogant officers, and sharp, fast-thinking commissars. After a short medical checkup, a quota of coal was assigned to each person. My quota was three hundred pounds per day. In case any man did not fill his quota, his small food ration was cut down, and in a short time he was resting in the cemetery.

I started concentrating on my escape. I knew that my subconscious mind would somehow find a way. My home in Germany was destroyed, my family wiped out; all my friends and former associates were either killed in the war or were in concentration camps.

I said to my subconscious mind, "I want to go to Los Angeles, and you will find the way." I had seen pictures of Los Angeles and I remembered some of the boulevards very well as well as some of the buildings.

Every day and night I would imagine I was walking down Wilshire Boulevard with an American girl whom I met in Berlin prior to the war (she is now my wife). In my imagination we would visit the stores, ride buses, and eat in the restaurants. Every night I made it a special point to drive my imaginary American automobile up and down the boulevards of Los Angeles. I made all this vivid and real. These pictures in my mind were as real and as natural to me as one of the trees outside the prison camp.

Every morning the chief guard would count the prisoners as they were lined up. He would call out "one, two, three," and so on, and when seventeen was called out, which was my number in sequence, I stepped aside. In the meantime, the guard was called away for a minute or so, and on his return he started by mistake on the next man as number seventeen. When the crew returned in the evening, the number of men was the same, and I was not missed, and the discovery would take a long time.

I walked out of the camp undetected and kept walking for twenty-four hours, resting in a deserted town the next day. I was able to live by fishing and killing some wildlife. I found coal trains going to Poland and traveled on them by night, until finally I reached Poland. With the help of friends, I made my way to Lucerne, Switzerland.

One evening at the Palace Hotel, Lucerne, I had a talk with a man and his wife from the United States of America. This man asked me if I would care to be a guest at his home in Santa Monica, California. I accepted, and when I arrived in Los Angeles, I found that their chauffeur drove me along Wilshire Boulevard and many other boulevards which I had imagined so vividly in the long months in the Russian coal mines. I recognized the buildings which I had seen in my mind so often. It actually seemed as if I had been in Los Angeles before. I had reached my goal.

I will never cease to marvel at the wonders of the subconscious mind. Truly, it has ways we know not of.

How Archaeologists and Paleontologists Reconstruct Ancient Scenes

Your subconscious mind has a memory of everything that has ever happened in the history of our species. Archaeologists studying ancient ruins and the countless artifacts left by the people of former cultures can put imaginative perception to marvelous use in their work. Their subconscious mind can aid them in reconstructing ancient scenes. The dead past becomes alive once more. Looking at the fragments of these ancient buildings and studying the pottery, statuary, tools, and household utensils of earlier civilizations, the scientist is able, through the common data banks of the universal mind, to know how, when, and why these objects were created.

The keen concentration and disciplined imagination of the scientist awakens the latent powers of the subconscious mind. This gives him the ability to clothe the ancient structures with roofs and surround them with gardens, pools, and fountains. The fossil remains are clothed with eyes, sinews, and muscles and they again walk and talk. The past becomes the living present, and we find that in mind there is no time or space. Through disciplined, controlled, and directed imagination, you can be a companion of the most scientific and inspired thinkers of all time.

How to Receive Guidance from Your Subconscious

When you have to make what you think will be a difficult decision, or when you fail to see the solution to your problem, begin at once to think constructively about it. If you are fearful and worried, you are not really thinking. True thinking is free from fear.

Here are the steps of a simple technique you can use to receive guidance on any subject:

- Quiet the mind and still the body. Tell the body to relax; it has to obey you. It has no volition, initiative, or self-conscious intelligence. Your body is an emotional disk that records your beliefs and impressions.

- Mobilize your attention; focus your thought on the solution to your problem.

- Try to solve it with your conscious mind.

- Think how happy you would be about the perfect solution. Sense the feeling you would have if the perfect answer were yours now.

- Let your mind play with this mood of happiness and contentment in a relaxed way; then drop off to sleep.

- When you awaken, if you do not have the answer, get busy

with something else. While you are preoccupied with something else, it is possible that the answer will pop into your mind.

In receiving guidance from the subconscious mind, the simple way is the best. Here is an illustration. I once lost a valuable ring that was a family heirloom. I looked everywhere for it, but it was nowhere to be found. I was worried and distressed by the loss.

That night I talked to my subconscious mind, in the same way that I would talk to anyone. Before dropping off to sleep, I said to it, "You know all things. You know where that ring is, and you now reveal to me where it is."

In the morning, I woke up suddenly with these words ringing in my ear: "Ask Robert!"

This seemed very strange to me. The only Robert I could think of offhand was the nine-year-old son of my next-door neighbors. Why should he know anything about the location of my ring? However, I followed the inner voice of intuition.

I found Robert in his yard and described the ring to him. "You haven't seen it, have you?" I asked.

"Oh, sure," he replied. "I found it in the bushes yesterday when I was playing hide-and-seek. I didn't know whose it was, so I took it inside and put it on my desk. I was going to put up a sign about it, but I forgot."

The subconscious mind will always answer you if you trust it.

A Lost Will

Hugo R. was a young man who attended my lectures in Los Angeles. He told me of his experience with the power of the subconscious mind. His father had died suddenly, apparently leaving no will. However, his sister told him that their father had once mentioned making his will and told her that he had done his best to make it fair to everyone.

Hugo realized that if his late father were ruled to have died intestate (without a will), the property would be divided up according to rules made by the state. It was not likely that this would fit their father's desires. Moreover, legal fees would consume much of the estate. He and his sister looked everywhere, but they could not locate the will. They began to wonder whether the will existed at all.

Then Hugo remembered what he had learned about using the subconscious mind. Before going to sleep, he talked to his deeper mind, saying, "I now turn this request over to the subconscious mind. It knows where my father's will is and reveals it to me." Then he condensed his request down to one word, "Answer." He repeated it over and over again, like a lullaby. He went to sleep with the word "Answer" echoing in his mind.

The next morning, he woke up with a tremendous urge to visit a certain bank in downtown Los Angeles. He wondered about this. Had he heard his father mention it once? Had he noticed a letter from the bank in his father's mail? He didn't know, but he did know that he had to check out this hunch. He went to the bank that morning. Eventually, a bank officer confirmed that there was a safe-deposit box in the vault registered in the name of his late father. When the box was opened, the missing will was discovered inside.

Your thought, as you go to sleep, arouses the powerful latency that is within you. Suppose you are wondering if you should sell your home, buy a certain stock, sever a partnership, move to New York or stay in Los Angeles, dissolve the present contract or take a new one. Do this: Sit quietly in your armchair or at the desk in your office. Remember that there is a universal law of action and reaction. The action is your thought. The reaction is the response from your subconscious mind. The subconscious mind is reactive and reflexive; that is its nature. It rebounds, rewards, and repays. It follows the law of correspondence. It responds by corresponding. As you contemplate right action, you will automatically experience a reaction or response in yourself that represents the guidance or answer of your subconscious mind.

In seeking guidance, you simply think quietly about right action. This means that you are using the Infinite Intelligence resident in the subconscious mind to the point where it begins to use you. From there on, your course of action is directed and controlled by the subjective wisdom within you, which is all-wise and omnipotent. Your decision will be right. There will be only right action because you are under a subjective compulsion to do the right thing. I use the word *compulsion* because the law of the subconscious is compulsion.

The Secret of Guidance

The secret of guidance or right action is to mentally devote yourself to the right answer until you find its response in you. The response is a feeling, an inner awareness, an overpowering hunch whereby you know that you know. You have used the power to the point where it begins to use you. You cannot possibly fail or make one false step while operating under the subjective wisdom within you. You will find that all your ways are pleasantness and all your paths are peace.

IDEAS TO REMEMBER

1. Remember that the subconscious mind has determined the success and wonderful achievements of all great scientific workers.

2. By giving your conscious attention and devotion to the solution of a perplexing problem, your subconscious mind gathers all the necessary information and presents it full-blown to the conscious mind.

3. If you are wondering about the answer to a problem, try to solve it objectively. Get all the information you can from research and also from others. If no answer comes, turn it over to your subconscious mind prior to sleep, and the answer always comes. It never fails.

4. You do not always get the answer overnight. Keep on turning your request over to your subconscious until the day breaks and the shadows flee away.

5. You delay the answer by thinking it will take a long time or that it is a major problem. Your subconscious has no problem, it knows only the answer.

6. Believe that you have the answer now. Feel the joy of the answer and the way you would feel if you had the perfect answer. Your subconscious will respond to your feeling.

7. Any mental picture, backed by faith and perseverance, will come to pass through the miracle-working power of your subconscious. Trust it, believe in its power, and wonders will happen as you pray.

8. Your subconscious is the storehouse of memory, and within your subconscious are recorded all your experiences since childhood.

9. Scientists meditating on ancient scrolls, temples, fossils, and other evidence are able to reconstruct scenes of the

past and make them alive today. Their subconscious mind comes to their aid.

10. Turn over your request for a solution to your subconscious prior to sleep. Trust it and believe in it, and the answer will come. It knows all and sees all, but you must not doubt or question its powers.

11. The action is your thought, and the reaction is the response of your subconscious mind. If your thoughts are wise, your actions and decisions will be wise.

12. Guidance comes as a feeling, an inner awareness, an overpowering hunch whereby you know that you know. It is an inner sense of touch. Follow it with the simplicity of faith.

Your subconscious mind answers you in ways you know not of. You may be led to a bookstore and pick up a book which answers your question, or you may overhear a conversation which provides the answer to your problem. The answer may come in countless and unexpected ways.

Chapter Thirteen

Your Subconscious Mind and the Wonders of Sleep

Your subconscious never sleeps. It is always on the job. It controls all your vital functions.

You spend about eight out of every twenty-four hours, or one third of your entire life, in sleep. This is an inexorable law of life. Sleep is a divine law, and many answers to our problems come to us when we are sound asleep.

Many people have advocated the theory that you get tired during the day, that you go to sleep to rest the body, and that a reparative process takes place while you sleep. This is a gross misunderstanding. Nothing rests in sleep. Your heart, lungs, and all your vital organs function while you are asleep. If you eat prior to sleep, the food is digested and assimilated. Your skin secretes perspiration. Your nails and hair continue to grow.

In the same way, your subconscious mind never rests or sleeps. It is always active, controlling all your vital forces.

The healing process takes place more rapidly while you are asleep, because there is no interference from your conscious mind. Remarkable answers are given to you while you are asleep.

Why We Sleep

One of the earliest scientific researchers to carry out serious investigations into sleep was Dr. John Bigelow. He was able to show that at night, while asleep, you receive constant impressions through the sensory nerves connected to the eyes, ears, and nose, and the subcutaneous nerves. The neural network of the brain is also quite active.

Dr. Bigelow's research led him to a conclusion that is closely aligned with the information presented in this book. He said that the main reason we sleep is in order that "the nobler part of the soul is united by abstraction to our higher nature and becomes a participant in the wisdom and foreknowledge of the gods."

Prayer and Meditation Are Forms of Sleep

Throughout the day, your conscious mind gets involved with vexations, strife, and contentions. It needs to be able to withdraw periodically from sense evidence and the objective world and commune silently with the inner wisdom of your subconscious mind. By claiming guidance, strength, and greater intelligence in all phases of your life, you will be enabled to overcome all difficulties and solve your daily problems.

This regular withdrawal from sense evidence and the noise and confusion of everyday living is also a form of sleep. That is, you become asleep to the world of the senses and alive to the wisdom and power of your subconscious mind.

Startling Effects of Sleep Deprivation

Lack of sleep can cause you to become irritable, moody, and depressed. All human beings need a minimum of six hours' sleep to be healthy. Most people need more. Those who think they can get along on less are fooling themselves.

Medical researchers who have investigated sleep processes and deprivation of sleep point out that severe insomnia has preceded psychotic breakdown in some instances.

Remember, you are spiritually recharged during sleep. Adequate sleep is essential to produce joy and vitality in life.

You Need More Sleep

One way to find out why we need sleep is to look at what happens when we do not get it. In 1964, a seventeen-year-old boy named Randy Gardner set out to win a place in the *Guinness Book of World Records*. He kept himself awake for 264 hours—eleven straight days! Later tests showed that he had suffered no permanent damage. However, during the time he was keeping himself awake, his thinking processes deteriorated. His speech became slurred. He suffered from memory lapses. In the later hours, he started to experience hallucinations.

Most people who are chronically short on sleep do not go to such extremes. However, they, too, may suffer from serious effects. According to the National Highway Traffic Safety Administration, as many as two hundred thousand traffic accidents a year are related to sleep problems. One driver in five has at least occasionally dozed off at the wheel. As a result, drivers are five to ten times more likely to have an accident late at night than during the daytime.

Experiments with volunteers have shown that a tired brain craves sleep so hungrily that it will sacrifice anything to get it.

After only a few hours of sleep loss, subjects start experiencing fleeting naps called "lapses" or microsleep. These happen three or four times an hour. During them, just as in "real" sleep, the person's eyelids close and his or her brain waves become slower.

At first, each of these lapses lasts just a fraction of a second, but as hours of sleep loss mount, the lapses take place more often and last longer, for as much as two or three seconds. Even if the subjects had been piloting an airliner in a thunderstorm, they still couldn't have resisted microsleep for those few priceless seconds.

Sleep Brings Counsel

Sandra F. is a young woman in Los Angeles who has often listened to my radio talks. She told me that she had been offered a position in New York City at twice her present salary. She could not decide whether or not to accept the new job. Before going to sleep, she prayed in these words:

> The creative intelligence of my subconscious mind knows what is best for me. Its tendency is always lifeward, and it reveals to me the right decision, which blesses me and all concerned. I give thanks for the answer that I know will come to me.

She repeated this simple prayer over and over as a lullaby as she drifted to sleep. In the morning, she had a persistent feeling that she should not accept the offer. She rejected it. Later events verified her inward sense of knowing. A few months after the job offer, the company went bankrupt.

The conscious mind may be correct on the objectively known facts. However, it was the intuitive faculty of the subconscious mind that realized the problems with the company and prompted her accordingly.

Saved from Certain Disaster

The wisdom of your subconscious mind can instruct you and protect you, if you pray for right action as you go to sleep.

Many years ago, I was offered a lucrative assignment in the Far East. I prayed for guidance and the right decision as follows:

> Infinite Intelligence within me knows all things. The right decision is revealed to me in divine order. I will recognize the answer when it comes.

I repeated this simple prayer over and over as a lullaby prior to sleep. That night, I had a dream in which an old friend came to me. He held out a newspaper and said, "Read these headlines! Do not go!" The headlines of the newspaper trumpeted stories of violence, unrest, and war—all of which occurred not long afterward in the area where I had been asked to go.

Your subconscious mind is all-wise. It knows all things. Often it will speak to you, but in a voice that your conscious mind will immediately accept. In the dream I just related, which doubtless saved me from putting myself in a situation of grave danger, my subconscious mind projected its warning in the guise of a person whom I trusted and respected.

To some, a warning may come in the form of a mother who appears in a dream. She tells the person not to go here or there, and the reason for the warning. Sometimes your subconscious will warn you in your waking hours. You think you hear a voice that sounds like that of your mother or some loved one. You stop and turn, looking for its source. Later you find that if you had gone on the way you were going, you might have been struck on the head by an object falling from a window.

Charge your subconscious with the task of evolving an answer to any problem prior to sleep and it will answer you.

Your subconscious is the storehouse of memory, and within your subconscious are recorded all your experiences since childhood.

Your Future Is Your Subconscious Mind

Remember that because your future is the result of your habitual thinking, it is already in your mind unless you change it through prayer. In the same way, the future of a country is in the collective subconscious of its people. There is nothing strange in the dream I had wherein I saw the headlines of the newspapers long before the events they spoke of. Those events had already taken place in the minds of those who would bring them about. All their plans were already engraved on that great recording instrument, the collective subconscious of the universal mind. Tomorrow's events are in your subconscious mind. So are next week's and next month's. They may be perceived by a highly psychic or clairvoyant person.

Nothing is predetermined or foreordained. Your mental attitude—the way you think, feel, and believe—determines your destiny. You can, through scientific prayer, mold, fashion, and create your own future. *Whatsoever a man soweth, that shall he also reap.*

A Catnap Nets Him $15,000

Years ago, one of my students mailed me a newspaper clipping about a man named Ray Hammerstrom who worked as a roller in a Pittsburgh steel mill. The mill had recently installed a new machine that controlled the delivery of newly forged steel bars to what were called cooling beds. Despite the best efforts of the installers, the machine could not be made to work properly. Engineers worked on it for several days, but to no avail.

Hammerstrom thought a lot about the problem. He tried to figure out a new design that might work. Nothing came to him. One afternoon he lay down for a nap. As he fell asleep, he thought about the switch problem. During his nap, he had a dream in which he saw a perfect design for the faulty switch. When he awoke, he sketched his new design according to the outline of his dream.

This visionary catnap won Hammerstrom a check for $15,000, the largest award the firm had ever given an employee for a new idea.

How a Professor Solved His Problem in Sleep

Dr. H. V. Helprecht was an eminent professor of Assyrian at the University of Pennsylvania. In his memoirs, he recounted an amazing experience:

> One Saturday evening I had been wearying myself, in the vain attempt to decipher two small fragments of agate, which were supposed to belong to the finger rings of some Babylonians.
>
> About midnight, weary and exhausted, I went to bed and dreamed the following remarkable dream: A tall, thin priest of Nippur, about forty years of age, led me to the treasure chamber of the temple . . . a small, low-ceilinged room without windows, while scraps of agate and lapis lazuli lay scattered on the floor. Here he addressed me as follows: "The two fragments which you have published separately on pages 22 and 26 belong together, are not finger rings. The first two rings served as earrings for the statue of the god; the two fragments [you

have] are the portions of them. If you will put them together you will have confirmation of my words." . . . I awoke at once . . . I examined the fragments . . . and to my astonishment found the dream verified. The problem was then at last solved.

This demonstrates clearly the creative manifestation of his subconscious mind, which knew the answer to all his problems.

How the Subconscious Worked for a Famous Writer While He Slept

In *Across the Plains*, Robert Louis Stevenson devotes a whole chapter to the topic of dreams. He was a vivid dreamer. It was his persistent habit to give specific instructions to his subconscious every night prior to sleep. He would request his subconscious to evolve stories for him while he slept. For example, if his bank account was low, his command to his subconscious would be something like this: "Give me a good thrilling novel that will be marketable and profitable." His subconscious responded magnificently.

Stevenson recounts:

These little brownies [the intelligences and powers of his subconscious] can tell me a story piece by piece, like a serial, and keep me, its supposed creator, all the while in total ignorance of where they aim.

That part of my work which is done when I am up and about [while he is consciously aware and awake] is by no means necessarily mine, since all goes to show that the brownies have a hand in it even then.

Sleep in Peace and Wake in Joy

If you suffer from insomnia, you will find the following prayer very effective. Repeat it slowly, quietly, and lovingly prior to sleep.

My toes are relaxed, my ankles are relaxed, my abdominal muscles are relaxed, my heart and lungs are relaxed, my hands and arms are relaxed, my neck is relaxed, my brain is relaxed, my face is relaxed, my eyes are relaxed, my whole mind and body are relaxed.

I fully and freely forgive everyone, and I sincerely wish for them harmony, health, peace, and all the blessings of life. I am at peace, I am poised, serene, and calm. I rest in security and in peace. A great stillness steals over me, and a great calm quiets my whole being as I realize the Divine Presence within me. I know that the realization of life and love heals me.

I wrap myself in the mantle of love and fall asleep filled with goodwill for all. Throughout the night peace remains with me, and in the morning I shall be filled with life and love. A circle of love is drawn around me. I will fear no evil, for thou art with me. I sleep in peace, I wake in joy, and in him I live, move, and have my being.

IDEAS TO REMEMBER

1. If you are worried that you will not wake up on time, suggest to your subconscious mind prior to sleep the exact time you wish to arise and it will awaken you. It needs no clock. Do the same thing with all problems. There is nothing too hard for your subconscious.

2. Forgive yourself and everyone else before you go to sleep and healing will take place much more rapidly.

3. Guidance is given you while you are asleep, sometimes in a dream. The healing currents are also released, and in the morning you feel refreshed and rejuvenated.

4. When troubled by the vexations and strife of the day, still the wheels of your mind and think about the wisdom

and intelligence lodged in your subconscious mind, which is ready to respond to you. This will give you peace, strength, and confidence.

5. Sleep is essential for peace of mind and health of body. Lack of sleep can cause irritation, depression, and mental disorders. You need eight hours' sleep.

6. Medical research scholars point out that insomnia sometimes precedes psychotic breakdowns.

7. You are spiritually recharged during sleep. Adequate sleep is essential for joy and vitality in life.

8. Your tired brain craves sleep so hungrily that it will sacrifice anything to get it. Many who have fallen asleep at the wheel of an automobile can testify to this.

9. Many sleep-deprived people have poor memories and lack proper coordination. They become befuddled, confused, and disorientated.

10. Sleep brings counsel. Prior to sleep, claim that the Infinite Intelligence of your subconscious mind is guiding and directing you. Then, watch for the lead that comes, perhaps on awakening.

11. Trust your subconscious completely. Know that its tendency is always lifeward. Occasionally, your subconscious answers you in a very vivid dream and a vision in the night. You can be forewarned in a dream in the same way as the author of this book was warned.

12. Your future is in your mind now, based on your habitual thinking and beliefs. Claim Infinite Intelligence leads and guides you and that all good is yours, and your fu-

ture will be wonderful. Believe it and accept it. Expect the best, and invariably the best will come to you.

13. If you are writing a novel, play, or book, or are working on an invention, speak to your subconscious mind at night and claim boldly that its wisdom, intelligence, and power are guiding, directing, and revealing to you the ideal play, novel, book or are revealing the perfect solution, whatever it may be. Wonders will happen as you pray this way.

Turn over your request for a solution to your subconscious mind prior to sleep. Trust it and believe in it, and the answer will come. It knows all and sees all, but you must not doubt or question its power.

Chapter Fourteen

Your Subconscious Mind and Marriage

Your mind marries many ideas. You marry beliefs, opinions, concepts, dogmas, theories, creeds; whatever you mentally and emotionally unite with in your mind, that's a marriage. Psychologically, your marriage partner is your idea, your concept of yourself, your estimate of yourself, your blueprint.

All marital trouble is caused by a failure to properly understand the functions and powers of the mind. Friction between husband and wife will disappear when each partner uses the law of mind correctly. By praying together they stay together. The contemplation of divine ideals, the study of the laws of life, the mutual agreement on a common purpose and plan, and the enjoyment of personal freedom bring about that harmonious marriage, that wedded bliss, that sense of oneness where the two become one.

The best time to prevent divorce is before marriage. There is nothing wrong with deciding to get out of a very bad situation. But why get into the bad situation in the first place? Would it not be better to give attention to the real cause of marital problems, to really get at the root of the matter in the first place?

The problems of marital unhappiness, discord, separation, and divorce are no different from all other problems of men and women. They can be traced directly to a lack of knowledge of the working and interrelationship of the conscious and subconscious mind.

The Meaning of Marriage

To be genuine, a marriage must begin on a sound spiritual basis. It must be of the heart, and the heart is the chalice of love. Honesty, sincerity, kindness, and integrity are all aspects of love. Each partner should be perfectly honest and sincere with the other. It is not a true marriage when a man marries a woman to lift his ego or because he wants to share her money or social position. This indicates a lack of sincerity, honesty, and true love. Such a marriage is a farce, a sham, and a masquerade.

If a woman says, "I am tired of working. I want to get married because I want security," her major premise is false. She is not using the laws of mind correctly. Her security depends upon her knowledge of the interaction of the conscious and subconscious mind and its application.

No person will lack for wealth or health if that person applies the techniques outlined in the chapters of this book. Wealth can come independent of her spouse, parents, or anyone else. No one is dependent on a spouse for health, peace, joy, inspiration, guidance, love, wealth, security, happiness, or anything in the world. Security and peace of mind come from knowledge of the powers within each of us and from the constant use of the laws of the mind in a constructive fashion.

How to Attract the Ideal Husband

If you have studied the chapters that precede this one, you are now acquainted with the way your subconscious mind works. You know that whatever you impress upon it will be experienced in your world. Begin now to impress your subconscious mind with the qualities and characteristics you desire in a man.

The following is an excellent technique: Sit down at night in your armchair, close your eyes, let go, relax the body, become very quiet, passive, and receptive. Talk to your subconscious mind and say to it:

I am now attracting a man into my experience who is honest, sincere, loyal, faithful, peaceful, happy, and prosperous. These qualities that I admire are sinking down into my subconscious mind now. As I dwell upon these characteristics, they become a part of me and are embodied subconsciously.

I know there is an irresistible law of attraction and that I attract to me a man according to my subconscious belief. I attract that which I feel to be true in my subconscious mind.

I know I can contribute to his peace and happiness. He loves my ideals, and I love his ideals. He does not want to make me over; neither do I want to make him over. There is mutual love, freedom, and respect.

Practice this process of impregnating your subconscious mind. Then, you will have the joy of attracting to you a man possessing the qualities and characteristics you mentally dwelt upon. Your subconscious intelligence will open up a pathway, whereby both of you will meet, according to the irresistible and changeless flow of your own subconscious mind. Have a keen desire to give the best that is in you of love, devotion, and cooperation. Be receptive to this gift of love which you have given to your subconscious mind.

How to Attract the Ideal Wife
To draw to yourself the life partner that you seek, affirm as follows:

> I now attract the right woman who is in complete accord with me. This is a spiritual union because it is divine love functioning through the personality of someone with whom I blend perfectly. I know I can give to this woman love, light, peace, and joy. I feel and believe I can make this woman's life full, complete, and wonderful.
>
> I now decree that she possesses the following qualities and attributes: She is spiritual, loyal, faithful, and true. She is harmonious, peaceful, and happy. We are irresistibly attracted to each other. Only that which belongs to love, truth, and beauty can enter my experience. I accept my ideal companion now.

As you think quietly and with deep interest on the qualities and attributes that you admire in the companion you seek, you will build the mental equivalent into your mentality. Then, the deeper currents of your subconscious mind will bring both of you together in divine order.

No Need for a Third Mistake
Recently Sheila B., a woman with many years of experience as an administrator, said to me, "I have had three husbands and all three have been passive and submissive. They all depended on me to make all decisions and govern everything. Why do I attract such men?"

I asked her if she had known before getting married the second time that her prospective husband had a similar character to her first husband.

"Of course not," she said emphatically. "If I had known he was such a milquetoast, I wouldn't have had anything to do with him. And the same goes for my third."

Sheila's trouble did not lie with the men she married. It was a result of her own personality makeup. She was a very assertive person with a strong need to stay in control of every situation she found herself in. On one level she wanted a partner who would be submissive and passive so that she could play the dominant role.

At the same time, her deeper need was for a partner who would be her equal. Her subconscious picture attracted to her the sort of man that she subjectively wanted, but once she found one, she discovered that he did not meet her real needs. She had to learn to break this pattern by adopting the right prayer process.

Breaking Negative Patterns

Sheila B. finally learned a simple truth. When you believe you can have the type of partner you idealize, it is done unto you as you believe.

To break the old subconscious pattern and attract to herself the ideal mate, Sheila used the following prayer:

I am building into my mentality the type of man I deeply desire. The man I attract for a husband is strong, powerful, loving, successful, honest, loyal, and faithful. He finds love and happiness with me. I love to follow where he leads.

I know he wants me, and I want him. I am honest, sincere,

loving, and kind. I have wonderful gifts to offer him. They are goodwill, a joyous heart, and a healthy body. He offers me the same. It is mutual. I give and I receive.

Divine Intelligence knows where this man is, and the deeper wisdom of my subconscious mind is now bringing both of us together in its own way, and we recognize each other immediately. I release this request to my subconscious mind which knows how to bring my request to pass. I give thanks for the perfect answer.

She prayed in this way every day, first thing in the morning and last thing before going to sleep. She affirmed these truths in the confident knowledge that through frequent occupation of the mind she would reach the mental equivalent of what she sought.

The Answer to Her Prayer

Several months went by. Sheila had a number of dates and social engagements, but none of the men she met was what she was looking for. She began to wonder if her quest was hopeless. She found herself starting to question, waver, doubt, and vacillate. At that point, she reminded herself that the Infinite Intelligence was bringing it to pass in its own way. There was nothing to be concerned about. When she received the final decree in her divorce proceedings, it brought her a great sense of release and mental freedom.

Soon afterward, she took a new position as head administrator in a medical group practice. The first day she was on the job, one of the senior physicians came by her office to introduce himself. He had been out of town at a medical conference the day she had interviewed for the position.

The minute he walked in, she knew he was the man she was praying for. Apparently he knew it, too. He proposed to her before a month had passed. Their subsequent marriage was ideally happy. This physician was not the passive or submissive type. He was strong, confident, and decisive. Well respected in his field, a former college athlete, he was also a deeply spiritual man.

Sheila got what she prayed for because she claimed it mentally until she reached the point of saturation. In other words, she mentally and emotionally united with her idea, and it became a part of her.

Honesty, sincerity, kindness, and integrity are also forms of love. Partners in love should be perfectly honest and sincere with each other.

If love is lacking in your life, use this prayer frequently: "God's love, wisdom, and harmony are being expressed through me now. Poise, balance, and equilibrium reign supreme in my life."

In love and marriage adjustments are needed, but this is not the same as trying to make your partner over. Such attempts only destroy the other's pride and self-esteem, and arouse a spirit of contrariness and resentment that proves fatal to the marriage bond.

Should I Get a Divorce?

Divorce is very much an individual question. There cannot be a general answer that is valid for everyone. In some cases, of course, there should never have been a marriage in the first place. In other cases, divorce is not a solution. Divorce may be right for one person and wrong for another. A person who is divorced may be far more sincere and noble than many married people who are perhaps living a lie.

For example, I was once consulted by a woman whose husband beat her and stole from her to support a drug habit. She had been brought up to believe that marriage is sacred and forever and that consequently divorce is immoral. I explained to her that true marriage is of the heart. If two hearts blend harmoniously, lovingly, and sincerely, that is the ideal marriage. The pure action of the heart is love.

Following this explanation she knew what to do. She knew in her heart that there is no divine law that compelled her to be browbeaten, intimidated, and beaten, simply because someone once said, "I pronounce you man and wife."

If you are in doubt as to what to do, ask for guidance. Know that there is always an answer and that you will receive it. Follow the lead that comes to you in the silence of your soul. It speaks to you in peace.

Drifting into Divorce

I once spoke with a young couple who had been married for only a few months but were already seeking a divorce. I discovered that the young man had a constant fear that his wife would leave him. He expected rejection and believed that she would be unfaithful to him. These thoughts haunted his mind and became an obsession with him.

His mental attitude was one of separation and suspicion. She felt unresponsive to him, but this was a result of his own feeling. The atmosphere of separation operating through his subconscious mind brought about a condition or action in accordance with the mental pattern behind it. There is a law of action and reaction, or cause and effect. The thought is the action, and the response of the subconscious mind is the reaction.

His wife left home and asked for a divorce—exactly what he had feared and believed she would do.

Divorce Begins in the Mind

Divorce takes place first in the mind; the legal proceedings follow after. These two young people were full of resentment, fear, suspicion, and anger. These attitudes weaken, exhaust, and debilitate the whole being. They learned that hate divides and that love unites. They began to realize what they had been doing with their minds. Neither of them knew the law of mental action. They were misusing their minds and bringing chaos and misery onto themselves.

At my suggestion, this couple got back together and experimented with prayer therapy. They began to radiate love, peace, and goodwill to each other. Each one practiced radiating harmony, health, peace, and love to the other, and they alternated in the reading of the Psalms every night. As a result of this sincere effort on their part, and the impregnation of their subconscious minds with beneficial impulses, their marriage is growing more beautiful every day.

The Nagging Wife

Many times the reason a wife nags is because she gets no attention. Her legitimate craving for love and affection expresses itself in a way that pushes her partner farther away. Give your wife attention, and show your appreciation. Praise and exalt all her many good points.

Another type of nagging reflects a desire to make the partner conform to a particular pattern. There are few quicker ways to drive a partner away. Wives and husbands must be on their guard not to be scavengers, always looking for petty faults or errors in each other. Let each give attention and praise for the constructive and wonderful qualities in the other.

The Brooding Husband

If a man begins to brood or grows morbid against his wife because of things she said or did, he is, psychologically speaking, committing adultery. One of the meanings of adultery is idolatry, which means giving attention to or uniting mentally with that which is negative and destructive. When a man is silently resenting his wife and is full of hostility toward her, he is unfaithful. He is not faithful to his marriage vows, which are to love, cherish, and honor her all the days of his life.

The man who is brooding, bitter, and resentful can swallow his sharp remarks, abate his anger, and go to great lengths to be considerate, kind, and courteous. He can deftly skirt the differences. Through praise and mental effort, he can get out of the habit of antagonism. As he soaks his subconscious mind with thoughts of peace, harmony, and love, he will find that he gets along better not only with his wife but with everyone in his life. Assume the harmonious state, and eventually you will find peace and harmony.

The Great Mistake

It is a great mistake to discuss your marital problems or difficulties with neighbors and relatives. Suppose, for example, a wife tells a neighbor, "John treats my mother abominably, drinks to excess, and is constantly abusive and insulting."

This wife is degrading and belittling her husband in the eyes of everyone she speaks to. Moreover, as she discusses and dwells upon the shortcomings of her husband, she is actually creating these states within herself. Who is thinking and feeling it? She is! And as you think and feel, so are you.

Relatives will usually give you the wrong advice. It is usually biased and prejudiced because it is not given in an impersonal way. Any advice you receive that violates the Golden Rule, which is a cosmic law, is not good or sound.

It is well to remember that no two human beings ever lived beneath the same roof without clashes of temperament, periods of hurt, and strain. Never display the unhappy side of your marriage to your friends. Keep your quarrels to yourself. Refrain from criticism and condemnation of your partner.

Don't Try to Remake Your Partner

Husbands and wives must not try to make their partners over into a second edition of themselves. The tactless attempt to change them is an affront, a statement that they are not worthy in themselves. These attempts are always foolish and many times lead to the destruction of the marriage. Attempting to alter someone destroys pride and self-esteem and arouses a spirit of contrariness and resentment that can prove fatal to the marriage bond.

Adjustments are needed, of course. None of us is perfect, and that holds for marriage partners as well. But if you have a good look inside your own mind and study your character and behavior, you will find enough shortcomings to keep you busy the rest of your life. If you think, "I will make him or her over into what I want," you are looking for trouble and the divorce court. You are asking for misery. You will have to learn the hard way that there is no one to change but yourself.

Pray Together and Stay Together

The first step: Never carry over from one day to another accumulated irritations arising from little disappointments. Be sure to forgive each other for any sharpness before you retire at night. The moment you awaken in the morning, claim Infinite Intelligence is guiding you in all your ways. Send out loving thoughts of peace, harmony, and love to your marriage partner, to all members of the family, and to the whole world.

The second step: Say grace at breakfast. Give thanks for the wonderful food, for your abundance, and for all your blessings. Make sure that no problems, worries, or arguments shall enter into the table conversation; the same applies at dinnertime. Say to your wife or husband, "I appreciate all you are doing, and I radiate love and goodwill to you all day long."

The third step: The husband and wife should alternate in praying each night. Do not take your marriage partner for granted. Show your appreciation and love. Think appreciation and goodwill, rather than condemnation, criticism, and nagging. The way to build a peaceful home and a happy marriage is to use a foundation of love, beauty, harmony, mutual respect, faith in God, and all things good. Before going to sleep read spiritual works and inspirational literature from the many religions and philosophies that have guided people through the ages. As you practice these truths, your marriage will grow more and more blessed through the years.

IDEAS TO REMEMBER

1. Ignorance of mental and spiritual laws is the cause of all marital unhappiness. By praying scientifically together, you stay together.

2. The best time to prevent divorce is before marriage. If you learn how to pray in the right way, you will attract the right mate for you.

3. Marriage is the union of a man and woman who are bound together by love. Their hearts beat as one, and they move onward, upward, and Godward.

4. Marriage does not guarantee happiness. People find happiness by dwelling on the eternal truths of God and the spiritual values of life. Then, the man and woman can contribute to each other's happiness and joy.

5. You attract the right mate by dwelling on the qualities and characteristics you admire in a woman or a man. Then your subconscious mind will bring you together in divine order.

6. You must build into your mentality the mental equivalent of what you want in a marriage partner. If you want to attract an honest, sincere, and loving partner in life, you must be honest, sincere, and loving yourself.

7. You do not have to repeat mistakes in marriage. When you really believe you can have the type of man or woman you idealize, it is done unto you as you believe. To believe is to accept something as true. Accept your ideal companion now mentally.

8. Do not wonder how, why, or where you will meet the mate you are praying for. Trust implicitly the wisdom of your subconscious mind. It has the power to carry out its mission. You don't have to assist it.

9. You are mentally divorced when you indulge in peeves, grudges, ill will, and hostility toward your marriage partner. You are mentally dwelling with error in your mind. Adhere to your marriage vows, "I promise to cherish, love, and honor him (or her) all the days of my life."

10. Cease projecting fear patterns to your marriage partner. Project love, peace, harmony, and goodwill, and your

marriage will grow more beautiful and more wonderful through the years.

11. Radiate love, peace, and goodwill to each other. These vibrations are picked up by the subconscious mind resulting in mutual trust, affection, and respect.

12. A nagging partner is usually seeking attention and appreciation. He or she is craving love and affection. Praise and exalt their many good points. Show them that you love and appreciate them.

13. Partners who love each other do not do anything unloving or unkind in word, manner, or action. Love is what love does.

14. In marital problems, always seek expert advice. You would not go to a carpenter to pull a tooth; neither should you discuss your marriage problems with relatives or friends. If you need counsel, go to a trained person.

15. Never try to make over your wife or husband. These attempts are always foolish and tend to destroy the pride and self-esteem of the other. Moreover, they arouse a spirit of resentment that can prove fatal to the marriage bond. Cease trying to make the other a second edition of yourself.

16. Pray together and you will stay together. Scientific prayer solves all problems. Mentally picture your wife as she ought to be, joyous, happy, healthy, and beautiful. See your husband as he ought to be, strong, powerful, loving, harmonious, and kind. Maintain this mental picture, and you will experience the marriage made in heaven, which is harmony and peace.

Every night of your life, pray together; then you'll stay together. Never carry over from one day to another irritations or disappointments. Be sure to forgive each other for any sharpness before you retire at night. The moment you awaken in the morning, claim Divine Intelligence is guiding you in all ways. Send out loving thoughts of peace and harmony and think of God and his love. Say, "Thank you, Father, for all the blessings of the day."

Chapter Fifteen

Your Subconscious Mind and Your Happiness

Start each day by saying to yourself: "Happiness will come to me. I have a sublime confidence in this power."

William James, the father of American psychology, said that the greatest discovery of the nineteenth century was not in the realm of physical science. The greatest discovery was the power of the subconscious touched by faith. In every human being is that limitless reservoir of power that can overcome any problem in the world.

True and lasting happiness will come into your life the day you get the clear realization that you can overcome any weakness—the day you realize that your subconscious can solve your problems, heal your body, and prosper you beyond your fondest dream.

You may have been very happy when you became engaged to the partner of your dreams. You may have felt happy when you graduated from college, when you got married, when your child was born, or when you won a great victory or a prize. You could go on and list other experiences that have made you happy.

However, no matter how marvelous these experiences are, they do not give real lasting happiness. They are transitory.

The Book of Proverbs gives the answer: *The happy man is he who trusts in the Lord*. When you trust in the Lord (the power and wisdom of your subconscious mind) to lead, guide, govern, and direct all your ways, you will become poised, serene, and relaxed. As you radiate love, peace, and goodwill to all, you are really building a superstructure of happiness for all the days of your life.

You Must Choose Happiness

Happiness is a state of mind. There is a phrase in the Bible that says, *Choose ye this day whom ye will serve*. You have the freedom to choose happiness. This may seem extraordinarily simple, and it is. Perhaps this is why people stumble on the way to happiness; they do not see the simplicity of the key to happiness. The great things of life are simple, dynamic, and creative. They produce well-being and happiness.

St. Paul reveals to you how you can think your way into a life of dynamic power and happiness in these words:

> *And now, my friends, all that is true, all that is noble, all that is just and pure, all that is lovable and gracious, whatever is excellent and admirable—fill all your thoughts with these things.* (Philippians 4:8)

How to Choose Happiness

Begin now to choose happiness. This is how you do it: When you open your eyes in the morning, say to yourself,

> Divine order takes charge of my life today and every day. All things work together for good for me today. This is a new

and wonderful day for me. There will never be another day like this one. I am divinely guided all day long, and whatever I do will prosper. Divine love surrounds me, enfolds me, and enwraps me, and I go forth in peace.

Whenever my attention wanders away from that which is good and constructive, I will immediately bring it back to the contemplation of that which is lovely and of good report. I am a spiritual and mental magnet attracting to myself all things that bless and prosper me. I am going to be a wonderful success in all my undertakings today. I am definitely going to be happy all day long.

Start each day in this manner; then you will be choosing happiness, and you will be a radiant, joyous person.

He Made It a Habit to Be Happy

A number of years ago, I stayed for about a week in a farmer's house in Connemarra on the west coast of Ireland. My host seemed always to be singing and whistling and was full of good humor. I asked him the secret of his happiness.

"Sure, it's a habit with me," he replied. "Every morning when I awaken and every night before I go to sleep, I bless my family, the crops, the cattle, and I thank God for the wonderful harvest."

This farmer had made a practice of this for over forty years. As you know, thoughts repeated regularly and systematically sink into the subconscious mind and become habitual. He discovered that happiness is a habit.

You Must Desire to Be Happy

There is one important point to remember about being happy. You must sincerely desire to be happy. There are people who have been depressed, dejected, and unhappy for so long that were they suddenly made happy by some wonderful, good, joyous news, they would react like the woman who once said to me, "It is wrong to be so happy!" They have become so accustomed to the old mental patterns that they do not feel at home being happy. They long to return to their familiar depressed, unhappy state.

I knew an elderly woman in England who had arthritis for many years. She would pat herself on the knee and say, "My arthritis is bad today. I can't possibly go out. My arthritis keeps me miserable." As a result of her condition, this woman got a lot of attention from her son, daughter, and neighbors. She really wanted her arthritis. She enjoyed her "misery," as she called it. On the level of her subconscious mind, she did not really want to be happy.

I suggested a curative procedure to her. I wrote down some biblical verses and told her that if she gave attention to these truths, her mental attitude would undoubtedly change. Her faith and confidence would be restored to health. She was not interested. Like many people, she suffered from a peculiar mental, morbid streak. She enjoyed being miserable and sad, or at least she enjoyed the benefits her misery brought her.

Why Choose Unhappiness?

Many people choose unhappiness without realizing that they are doing so. They do so by entertaining such ideas as these:

- Today is a black day; everything is going to go wrong.

- I am not going to succeed.

- Everyone is against me.

- Business is bad, and it is going to get worse.

- I'm always late.

- I never get the breaks.

- He can, but I can't.

If you have this attitude of mind the first thing in the morning, you will attract all these experiences to you, and you will be very unhappy.

Begin to realize that the world you live in is determined largely by what goes on in your mind. Marcus Aurelius, the great Roman philosopher and sage, said, "A man's life is what his thoughts make of it." The leading American philosopher of the nineteenth century, Ralph Waldo Emerson, said, "A man is what he thinks all day long." The thoughts you habitually entertain in your mind have the tendency to actualize themselves in physical conditions.

Make certain you do not indulge in negative, defeatist, or unkind, depressing thoughts. Recall frequently to your mind that you can experience nothing outside your own mentality.

If I Had a Million Dollars . . .

Wealth in and of itself will not make you happy. On the other hand, it is not a deterrent to happiness. Today, many people try to buy happiness by buying things—a high-definition television, the latest car, expensive designer clothes, a house in the country. But happiness cannot be purchased or procured in that way.

The kingdom of happiness is in your thought and feeling. Too many people have the idea that it takes something artificial to produce happiness. Some say, "If I were elected mayor, made CEO of the corporation, featured on the society page of the paper, I would be happy."

The truth is that happiness is a mental and spiritual state. A promotion or external honor will not yield happiness. Your strength, joy, and happiness consist in finding out the law of divine order and right action lodged in your subconscious mind and applying these principles in all phases of your life.

You can rise victorious over any defeat and find happiness through the marvelous power of your subconscious mind.

You cannot buy happiness. The kingdom of happiness is in your thought and feeling.

The happiest people are those that bring forth the best in themselves.

Happiness Is the Harvest of a Quiet Mind

When I was lecturing in San Francisco some years ago, I was approached by a man who was very unhappy and dejected over the way his business was going. He was the general manager of a corporation. His heart was filled with resentment toward the vice president and the president of the company. He felt that their opposition to his ideas was leading the company in a terrible direction. Profits were declining, as was market share. The company's share price was also going down, which concerned him greatly because much of his compensation was in the form of stock options.

This is how he solved his business problem: The first thing each morning he affirmed quietly as follows:

All those working in our corporation are honest, sincere, co-operative, faithful, and full of goodwill to all. They are mental and spiritual links in the chain of this corporation's growth, welfare, and prosperity. I radiate love, peace, and goodwill in my thoughts, words, and deeds to my two associates and to all those in the company.

The president and the vice president of our company are divinely guided in all their undertakings. The Infinite Intelligence of my subconscious mind makes all decisions through me. There is only right action in all our business transactions and in our relationship with each other.

I send the messengers of peace, love, and goodwill before me to the office. Peace and harmony reign supreme in the minds and hearts of all those in the company, including myself. I now go forth into a new day, full of faith, confidence, and trust.

This business executive repeated the preceding meditation slowly three times in the morning, feeling the truth of what he affirmed. When fearful or angry thoughts came into his mind during the day, he would say to himself, "Peace, harmony, and poise govern my mind at all times."

As he continued disciplining his mind in this manner, all the harmful thoughts ceased to come, and peace came into his mind. He reaped the harvest.

Subsequently, he wrote me to the effect that at the end of about two weeks of reordering his mind, the president and the vice president called him into the office, praised his operations and his new constructive ideas, and remarked how fortunate they were in having him as general manager. He was very happy in discovering that man finds happiness within himself.

The Block Is in the Mind

Years ago a friend told me the story of a horse that had been frightened by a snake next to a stump on the road. From then on, every time the horse came to that same stump, he shied. The farmer dug the stump out, burned it, and leveled the road. It didn't help. For years afterward, every time the horse passed the place where the stump had been, he shied. The horse was shying at the *memory* of a stump.

There is no block to your happiness save in your own thought life and mental imagery. Are fear or worry holding you back? Fear is a thought in your mind. You can dig it up this moment by supplanting it with faith in success, achievement, and victory over all problems.

I knew a man whose business went bankrupt. He said to me, "I made mistakes, but I've learned a lot from them. I am going back into business, and I will be a tremendous success." He faced up to that stump in his mind. He did not whine or complain. Instead, he dug up the stump of failure. Through believing in his inner powers to back him up, he banished all fear thoughts and old depressions. Believe in yourself, and you will succeed and be happy.

The Happiest People

The happiest person is the one who constantly brings forth and practices what is best in himself or herself. Happiness and virtue complement each other. Not only are the best the happiest, but the happiest are usually the best in the art of living life successfully. God is the highest and best in you. Express more of God's love, light, truth, and beauty, and you will become one of the happiest persons in the world today.

Epictetus, the Greek stoic philosopher, said:

There is but one way to tranquility of mind and happiness; let this, therefore, be always ready at hand with thee, both when thou wakest early in the morning, and all the day long, and when thou goest late to sleep, to account no external things thine own, but commit all these to God.

IDEAS TO REMEMBER

1. William James said that the greatest discovery of the nineteenth century was the power of the subconscious mind touched by faith.

2. There is tremendous power within you. Happiness will come to you when you acquire a sublime confidence in this power. Then you will make your dreams come true.

3. You can rise victorious over any defeat and realize the cherished desires of your heart through the marvelous power of your subconscious mind. This is the meaning of *Whosoever trusts in the Lord* [spiritual laws of the subconscious mind], *happy is he.*

4. You must choose happiness. Happiness is a habit. It is a good habit on which to ponder often.

5. When you open your eyes in the morning, say to yourself, "I choose happiness today. I choose success today. I choose right action today. I choose love and goodwill for all today. I choose peace today." Pour life, love, and interest into this affirmation, and you have chosen happiness.

6. Give thanks for all your blessings several times a day. Furthermore, pray for the peace, happiness, and prosperity of the members of your family, your associates, and all people everywhere.

7. You must sincerely desire to be happy. Nothing is accomplished without desire. Desire is a wish with wings of imagination and faith. Imagine the fulfillment of your desire, feel its reality, and it will come to pass. Happiness comes in answered prayer.

8. By constantly dwelling on thoughts of fear, worry, anger, hate, and failure, you will become depressed and unhappy. Remember, your life is what your thoughts make of it.

9. You cannot buy happiness with all the money in the world. Some millionaires are happy, some are unhappy. Many people with little worldly wealth are happy, and some are unhappy. Some married people are happy, and some unhappy. Some single people are happy, and some are unhappy. The kingdom of happiness is in your thought and feeling.

10. Happiness is the harvest of a quiet mind. Anchor your thoughts on peace, poise, security, and divine guidance, and your mind will be productive of happiness.

11. There is no block to your happiness. External things are not causative. They are effects, not causes. Take your cue from the only creative principle within you. Your thought is cause, and a new cause produces a new effect. Choose happiness.

12. The happiest person is the one who brings forth the highest and the best in himself or herself.

Remember, your subconscious mind cannot act if your mind is divided. You cannot find happiness if you are harboring thoughts of doubt that lasting happiness will ever be yours.

Chapter Sixteen

Your Subconscious Mind and Harmonious Human Relations

You have the freedom to make your own choices. Take a personal inventory of the contents of your mind, then choose thoughts of health, happiness, peace, and abundance and you will reap fabulous dividends in all your relationships.

A vital concept you have learned from studying this book is that your subconscious mind is like a recording machine that faithfully reproduces whatever you impress upon it. This is one of the reasons the Golden Rule is so central to creating and maintaining a harmonious balance in your relationships with others.

> *Always treat others as you would like them to treat you.*
> (Matthew 7:12)

This lesson from Matthew has both outer and inner meanings. The inner meaning concerns the connection between your conscious and subconscious mind.

- As you would want people to think about you, think you about them in like manner.

- As you would want people to feel about you, feel you also about them in like manner.

- As you would want people to act toward you, act you toward them in like manner.

For example, you may be polite and courteous to someone in your office, but when her back is turned, you are very critical and resentful toward her in your mind. Such negative thoughts are highly destructive to you. It is like taking poison. The negative energy you are generating robs you of vitality, enthusiasm, strength, guidance, and goodwill. As these negative thoughts and emotions sink into your subconscious, they cause all kinds of difficulties and maladies in your life.

The Master Key to Happy Relations

Pass no judgment, and you will not be judged. For as you judge others, so you will yourselves be judged, and whatever measure you deal out to others will be dealt back to you. (Matthew 7:1–2)

The key to harmonious relations with others lies in the close study of these verses and the application of the inner truths they represent. To judge is to think, to arrive at a mental verdict or conclusion in your mind. The thought you have about the other person is *your* thought, because *you* are thinking it. Your thoughts are creative. Therefore, you actually create in your own experience what you think and feel about the other person. The suggestion you give to another, you give to yourself as well, because your mind is the creative medium.

This is why it is said, *For as you judge others, so will you yourselves be judged.* This means that in applying standards and criteria to others, you create those standards and criteria in your subconscious, which then applies them to you. Once you know this law and understand the way your subconscious mind works, you will always be careful to think, feel, and act right toward others, for in doing so you are creating a situation of right action, feeling, and thought toward yourself.

And whatever measure you deal out to others will be dealt back to you. The good you do for others comes back to you in like measure; and the evil you do returns to you by the law of your own mind. If someone cheats and deceives another, he is actually cheating and deceiving himself: His sense of guilt and mood of loss inevitably will attract loss to him in some way, at some time. His subconscious records his mental act and reacts according to the mental intention or motivation.

Your subconscious mind is impersonal and unchanging, neither considering persons nor respecting religious affiliations or institutions of any kind. It is neither compassionate nor vindictive. The way you think, feel, and act toward others returns at last upon yourself.

The Daily Headlines Made Him Sick

Begin now to observe yourself. Observe your reactions to people, conditions, and circumstances. Record them in a notebook for later study. How do you respond to the events and news of the day? It makes no difference if all the other people were wrong and you alone were right. If the news disturbs you, it is your evil because your negative emotions robbed you of peace and harmony.

A woman wrote me to ask for help with her husband. She explained that he went into a rage every time he read what certain columnists wrote in the newspaper. She added that this constant reaction of anger and suppressed rage on his part was very bad for his high blood pressure. His doctor had told him that he had to find some way to reduce his stress through emotional reconditioning.

I invited this man to come see me. I explained to him the way his mind functions. He understood that it was emotionally immature to get angry over an article in the newspaper, but he had not known the damage his anger was causing to his own mind and body.

He began to realize that he should give the columnist the freedom to express himself even if he disagreed with him politically, religiously, or in any other way. In the same manner, the columnist ought to give him the freedom to write a letter to the newspaper disagreeing with his published statements. He learned that he could disagree without being disagreeable. He awakened to the simple truth that it is never what some other person says or does that affects him. Rather, it is his own reaction to what is said or done that matters.

This explanation helped this man achieve a cure. He realized that with a little practice he could master his morning tantrums. His wife later told me that he eventually learned to laugh at what the columnists he so disliked had to say. He also learned to laugh at himself for reacting so strongly. The newspaper articles no longer have power to disturb, annoy, and irritate him. His hypertension is more under control as a result of his increased emotional poise and serenity.

I Hate Women, But I Like Men

Cynthia R. was an executive secretary with a large corporation. She came to me because she felt very bitter toward some of the women in her office. She believed they were gossiping and, as she said, spreading vicious lies about her. When I asked, she admitted that she had many problems in her relationships with other women. She said, "I hate women, but I like men."

As I continued to talk with her, I discovered that Cynthia spoke to the people she supervised in a very haughty, imperious, and irritable tone of voice. There was a certain pomposity in her way of speaking, and I could see where her tone of voice would affect some people unpleasantly. She did not realize this. For her, the important point was that her coworkers took delight in making things difficult for her.

If all the people in your office or factory annoy you, isn't it possible that this annoyance and turmoil may be due to some subconscious pattern or mental projection that is coming from you? We all know that a dog will react ferociously if you hate or fear dogs. Animals pick up your subconscious vibrations and react accordingly. Is it so outrageous to say that human beings are just as sensitive as dogs, cats, and other animals in this regard?

To this woman who hated women, I suggested a process of prayer. I explained to her that when she began to identify herself with spiritual values and commenced to affirm the truths of life, her hatred of women would completely disappear, along with the vocal patterns and mannerisms that communicated that hatred to others. She was surprised to learn that our emotions show up in our speech, actions, writings, and in all phases of our life.

As a result of our conversation, Cynthia stopped behaving in her typical resentful and angry way. She established a pattern of prayer that she practiced regularly, systematically, and conscientiously in the office.

This was the prayer she used with such success:

I think, speak, and act lovingly, quietly, and peacefully. I now radiate love, peace, tolerance, and kindliness to all those who criticized me and gossiped about me. I anchor my thoughts on peace, harmony, and goodwill to all.

Whenever I am about to react negatively, I say firmly to myself, "I think, speak, and act from the standpoint of the principle of harmony, health, and peace within myself." Creative intelligence leads, rules, and guides me in all my ways.

The practice of this prayer transformed her life. She found that the atmosphere of criticism and annoyance in her workplace gradually disappeared. Her coworkers became friends and companions in life's journey. She discovered the truth, that we have no one to blame and no one to change but ourselves.

His Inner Speech Held Back His Promotion

One day Jim S., a sales representative, came to see me. He was deeply upset by the difficulties he had working with the sales manager of his organization. Jim had been with the company ten years without receiving any promotion or recognition of any kind. He showed me his sales figures. I could easily see that they were higher proportionately than those of the other sales representatives in the territory. His explanation was that the sales manager did not like him. He claimed that he was unjustly treated. At conferences the manager ridiculed his suggestions and at times was actively rude to him.

After discussing his situation in greater detail, I suggested to Jim that the cause was to a great degree within himself. The reaction of his superior bore witness to Jim's concept and belief about this man. The measure we mete shall be measured to us again. Jim's mental measure or concept of the sales manager was that he was mean, prejudiced, and cantankerous. Jim was filled with bitterness and hostility toward the executive. On his way to work he conducted a vigorous conversation with himself filled with criticism, mental arguments, recriminations, and denunciations of his sales manager.

What Jim gave out mentally, he was inevitably bound to get back. By the end of our conversation, Jim realized that his inner speech was highly destructive. The intensity and force of his silent thoughts and emotions, the mental condemnation and vilification of the sales manager that he rehearsed, entered into his own subconscious mind. This brought about the negative response from his boss, as well as creating other personal, physical, and emotional disorders.

At my urging, Jim began to pray frequently as follows:

> I am the only thinker in my universe. I am responsible for what I think about my boss. My sales manager is not responsible for the way I think about him. I refuse to give power to any person, place, or thing to annoy me or disturb me. I wish health, success, peace of mind, and happiness for my boss. I sincerely wish him well, and I know he is divinely guided in all his ways.

He repeated this prayer out loud slowly, quietly, and feelingly, knowing that his mind is like a garden and that whatever he plants in the garden will come forth like seeds after their kind.

I also taught him to practice visualization or mental imagery prior to sleep. He created a scenario in which his superior congratulated him on his fine work, praised his zeal and enthusiasm, and remarked on the wonderful response he obtained from customers. He felt the reality of all this. He felt his boss's handshake, heard the tone of his voice, and saw him smile. He made a real mental movie, dramatizing it to the best of his ability. Night after night he replayed this mental movie, knowing that his subconscious mind was the receptive medium on which his conscious imagery would be impressed.

Gradually, by a process of what we can think of as mental and spiritual osmosis, the impression was made on his subconscious mind. The expression automatically came forth. Jim's sales manager subsequently called him up to San Francisco, congratulated him, and gave him a promotion to division sales manager, with greatly increased responsibilities and a substantial raise in salary. Once Jim changed his concept and estimate of his boss, his subconscious mind saw to it that his boss responded accordingly.

> *Give no one in all the world the power to deflect you from your goal, your aim in life, which is to express your hidden talents to the world, to serve humanity, and to reveal more and more of God's wisdom, truth, and beauty to all people in the world.*
>
> *Love is the answer to getting along with others. Love is understanding, goodwill, and a respect for the divinity of the other.*

Becoming Emotionally Mature

What someone else says cannot really annoy or irritate you unless you *permit* it to disturb you. The only path by which another person can upset you is through your own thought. If you get angry, you have to go through four stages in your mind. You begin to think about what was said. You decide to get angry and generate an emotion of rage. Then you decide to act. Perhaps you talk back and react in kind. As you see, the thought, emotion, reaction, and action all take place in your own mind.

What does it mean to be emotionally mature? It means that you move beyond the natural, but childish, tendency to respond negatively to the criticism and resentment of others. No one likes to be criticized or belittled. However, we have the ability to choose how to react when it happens. The mature choice is to refrain from responding in a similarly negative way. Responding in kind means to descend to the level of belittling criticism and to become one with the negative atmosphere of the other. Identify yourself with your own aim in life. Do not permit any person, place, or thing to deflect you from your inner sense of peace, tranquility, and radiant health.

The Meaning of Love

Sigmund Freud, the founder of psychoanalysis and one of the most important figures in the history of psychology, said that unless the personality has love, it sickens and dies. Love includes understanding, goodwill, and respect for the divinity in the other person. The more love and goodwill you emanate and exude, the more comes back to you.

If you puncture someone else's ego and wound her estimate of herself, you cannot gain her goodwill. Recognize that everyone wants to be loved and appreciated. Everyone needs to feel important in the world. Realize that the other person is conscious of her true worth. Like yourself, she feels the dignity of being an expression of the one life-principle animating all people. As you do this consciously and knowingly, you build up the other person, and she returns your love and goodwill.

She Hated Her Audiences

Marie C. had always dreamed of being an actress. She studied theater in college, then had the good fortune to be hired by an important regional theater company in a part of the country she did not know at all. The first time she performed with the company, the audience booed her. Dismayed and angry, she decided that the people of that region were stupid, ignorant, and backward. She hated them all. After a miserable time, she was dropped from the company. She moved back to the area where she had grown up, and left the stage to work as a waitress.

One day a friend invited her to go to a lecture in Town Hall in New York City. The topic was "How to Get Along with Ourselves." This lecture changed her life. She began to see that she had overreacted to her early experience with the regional company. She admitted to herself that the play she had been in that first time was not good and that, as a new member of the company, she had probably not been at her best. The fault did not lie with the people in the audience, but with the way she accepted their reaction, then turned it back on them in the form of negative energy.

Marie decided to return to the stage and to her lifelong dream of being an actress. She began to pray sincerely for the audience and for herself. She poured out love and goodwill every night before stepping onto the stage. She made it a habit to claim that the peace of God filled the hearts of all present and that all present were lifted up and inspired. During each performance she sent out love vibrations to the audience. Today, she has an important career in theater. She transmits her goodwill and esteem to others, and they return it in kind.

Handling Difficult People

It should not come as a surprise that some people in the world are difficult. They are twisted and distorted mentally. They are malconditioned. Many are mental delinquents who have become argumentative, uncooperative, cantankerous, cynical, and sour on life. They are sick psychologically. Their minds have become deformed and distorted, perhaps because of experiences they have had in the past.

What do you do when you have to deal with someone like this? The temptation is to turn their negative energy back on them in the form of dislike. But to do that, you first have to take their negativity into yourself, with all the bad effects that will have on your own being. Strive instead to "return good for evil." This creates an armor that keeps their difficult and unpleasant attitudes from affecting you, and your transmission of compassion and understanding will set in motion the process of changing them.

Misery Loves Company

The hateful, frustrated, distorted, and twisted personality is out of tune with the infinite. The person resents those who are peaceful, happy, and joyous. Usually he criticizes, condemns, and vilifies those who have been very good and kind to him. His attitude is this: Why should they be so happy when I am so miserable? He wants to drag them down to his own level. The old saying that "misery loves company" is still true. Once you understand this, you remain unmoved, calm, and dispassionate.

A man named Bruce T. who attended my lectures in London told me of his experience with this process. He had become active in a volunteer organization that was concerned with beautifying the community where he lived. Most of the volunteers were genuinely interested in working on planting, gardens, sprucing up rundown areas, and repairing dilapidated buildings. One member, however, opposed every measure that anyone suggested. More than that, he constantly attacked the motives of the others. He made the meetings of the group so unpleasant that attendance began to decline.

Some of the other members came to Bruce. They suggested that they band together and expel the grouch from the organization. He was about to go along with this plan when he realized that to do so would be to perpetuate the man's twisted attitudes within himself. Instead, he began to visualize the man changing into a pleasant, cooperative member of the group. Before each meeting, Bruce went into a quiet corner and repeated:

> I think, speak, and act in true accord with the principle of harmony and peace within myself. All who bind themselves to the goals of our organization do so with kindness and purpose in Divine Order. There is no discord, no unpleasantness. Creative intelligence leads, rules, and guides us in all we do.

After several weeks, the man who had caused so much trouble proposed a new initiative. He presented it in such an agreeable and cooperative manner that he won the approval of everyone else in the organization, including those who had wanted to kick him out.

The Practice of Empathy

A young woman named Alice O. visited me recently. She told me that she had long hated another young woman in the office where she worked. Her reason was that the other woman was prettier, happier, and more prosperous than she. The crowning blow came when the other woman became engaged to marry the CEO of the company, whom Alice had long admired.

One day after the marriage took place, the woman she so disliked came into work with her daughter from a previous marriage. Alice had not known her coworker had a child or even that she had been married before. Because of a congenital problem, the woman's daughter wore a steel leg brace. Alice overheard her say to her mother, "Mommy, is this where my new daddy works, too? I love this place, because it is so full of people I love."

"My heart suddenly went out to that little girl," Alice told me. "I knew how happy she must feel. I got a vision of how happy this woman was, against odds I had not even known about. All of a sudden I felt love for her. I went into her office and wished her all the happiness in the world. And I meant it."

In that moment, Alice experienced what psychologists call *empathy*. This is not the same thing as sympathy, in which we understand the feelings of others. It is more. It means imaginatively projecting yourself into the mental attitudes and states of the other person. When Alice projected her mental mood or the feeling of her heart into that of the other woman, it was as if she began to think through the other woman's experience. She was thinking and feeling as the other woman, and also as the child, because she had also projected herself into the mind of the child.

Any time you feel tempted to injure or think ill of another, project yourself mentally into his or her mind. Sense what that person senses, feel what that person feels, think as that person thinks and you will feel the truth of the words *Love ye one another.*

Appeasement Never Wins

Do not permit people to take advantage of you and gain their point by temper tantrums, crying jags, or other forms of emotional blackmail. These people are dictators who try to enslave you and make you do their bidding. Be firm but kind, and refuse to yield. Appeasement never wins. Refuse to contribute to their delinquency, selfishness, and possessiveness. Remember, do that which is right. You are here to fulfill your ideal and remain true to the eternal verities and spiritual values of life, which are eternal.

Remain true to your ideal. Know definitely and absolutely

that whatever contributes to your peace, happiness, and fulfill-ment must of necessity bless all people who walk the earth. The harmony of the part is the harmony of the whole; for the whole is in the part, and the part is in the whole. All you owe the other is love, and love is the fulfilling of the law of health, happiness, and peace of mind.

IDEAS TO REMEMBER

1. Your subconscious mind is a recording machine that re-produces your habitual thinking. Think good of the other, and you are actually thinking good about yourself.

2. A hateful or resentful thought is a mental poison. Do not think ill of another for to do so is to think ill of yourself. You are the only thinker in your universe, and your thoughts are creative.

3. Your mind is a creative medium; therefore, what you think and feel about the other, you are bringing to pass in your own experience. This is the psychological meaning of the Golden Rule. As you would that others should think about you, think you about them in the same manner.

4. To cheat, rob, or defraud another brings lack, loss, and limitation to yourself. Your subconscious mind records your inner motivations, thoughts, and feelings. When these are negative, loss, limitation, and trouble come to you in countless ways. What you do to the other, you are doing to yourself.

5. The good you do, the kindness proffered, the love and good you send forth will all come back to you multiplied in many ways.

6. You are responsible for the way you think about the other. Remember, the other person is not responsible for the way you think about him or her. Your thoughts are reproduced. What are you thinking now about the other person?

7. Become emotionally mature and permit other people to differ with you. They have a perfect right to disagree with you, and you have the same freedom to disagree with them. You can disagree without being disagreeable.

8. Just as animals are able to pick up fear vibrations, many people are just as sensitive. The thoughts you believe are hidden are actually broadcast by your voice, your facial expressions, and your body language. This is true both for positive and negative thoughts.

9. Your inner speech, representing your silent thoughts and feelings, is experienced in the reactions of others toward you.

10. Wish for the other what you wish for yourself. This is the key to harmonious human relations.

11. Change your concept and estimate of your employer. Feel and know he or she is practicing the Golden Rule and the law of love, and he or she will respond accordingly.

12. Another person cannot annoy you or irritate you except if you permit him or her to. Your thought is creative; you can bless the other person. If someone calls you an insulting name, you have the freedom to reply, "God's peace fills your soul."

13. Love is the answer to getting along with others. Love is understanding, goodwill, and a respect for the divinity of the other.

14. Have compassion and understanding for those whose negative conditioning has made them difficult and unpleasant. The divine spark is within them, just as it is within everyone. To understand all is to forgive all.

15. Rejoice in the success, promotion, and good fortune of others. In doing so, you attract good fortune to yourself.

16. Never yield to another's emotional scenes and tantrums. Appeasement never wins. Do not be a doormat. Adhere to that which is right. Stick to your ideal, knowing that the mental outlook that gives you peace, happiness, and joy is right, good, and true. What blesses you, blesses all.

17. All you owe any person in the world is love, and love is wishing for everyone what you wish for yourself—health, happiness, and all the blessings of life.

Become emotionally mature and permit other people to differ with you. They have a perfect right to disagree with you, and you have the same freedom to disagree with them. You can disagree without being disagreeable.

Chapter Seventeen

How to Use Your Subconscious Mind for Forgiveness

The true meaning of forgiveness is to forgive yourself. Forgiveness is getting your thoughts in line with the divine law of harmony. Self-condemnation is called hell (bondage and restriction); forgiveness is called heaven (harmony and peace).

Life plays no favorites. God is life, and this life-principle is flowing through you at this moment, as you read and think upon these words. God loves to express himself through you as harmony, peace, beauty, joy, and abundance. This is called the will of God or the tendency of life.

If you set up resistance in your mind to the flow of life through you, this emotional congestion will snarl up your subconscious mind and cause all kinds of negative conditions. God has nothing to do with the unhappy or chaotic conditions in the world. All these conditions are brought about by the negative and destructive thinking of our species. Therefore, it is a serious mistake to blame God for your trouble or sickness.

Many persons habitually set up mental resistance to the flow of life by accusing and reproaching God for the sin, sickness, and suffering of mankind. Others cast the blame on God for their pains, aches, loss of loved ones, personal tragedies, and accidents. They are angry at God, and they believe he is responsible for their misery.

As long as people entertain such negative concepts about God, they will experience automatic negative reactions from their subconscious minds. What they fail to understand is that they are punishing themselves. They must see the truth, find release, and give up all condemnation, resentment, and anger against anyone or any power outside themselves. Otherwise, they cannot go forward into a healthy, happy, or creative activity. At the instant these people entertain a God of love in their minds and hearts, at the instant they believe that God is a loving Father who watches over them, cares for them, guides them, sustains and strengthens them, this concept and belief about God or the life-principle will be accepted by their subconscious mind, and they will find themselves blessed in countless ways.

Life Always Forgives You
The life-principle holds a bottomless fund of forgiveness for you. It forgives you when you cut your finger. The subconscious intelligence within you sets about immediately to repair it. New cells build bridges over the cut. If you contract an infection from a harmful organism, life forgives you and sets about surrounding and annihilating the invader. If you burn your hand, the life-principle reduces the edema and congestion and gives you new skin, tissue, and cells.

Life holds no grudges against you. It is always forgiving you. Life brings you back to health, vitality, harmony, and peace, if you cooperate by thinking in harmony with nature. Negative, hurtful memories, bitterness, and ill will clutter up and impede the free flow of the life-principle within you.

Banishing Guilt

Harriet G. worked late at the office every day. She often did not go home until after midnight. She expected that her superiors and coworkers would pat her on the back because she worked so hard. They didn't. Since she was usually the only one who stayed so late, the others didn't even know about her unusual devotion. Meanwhile, her family life was in serious trouble. Her husband and two sons hardly knew what she looked like. When her younger son's Little League team made the local playoffs, Harriet not only missed the game but she also forgot to ask who won. To top it off, Harriet's doctor warned her that she was developing dangerously high blood pressure.

Harriet came to talk to me after her husband told her he wanted a separation. I asked her why she shut her husband out of her life and showed so little interest in her boys. At first she tried to say that she had to work so hard just to keep up with her job. I asked if her coworkers put in as much time as she did. No, she admitted, the others in her company kept pretty normal hours, and they were not any better at the job than she was.

I suggested to her why she was working so arduously.

"There is something eating you inside," I told her. "If there weren't, you would not act this way. You are punishing yourself for something."

For a while, she resisted this suggestion. She kept trying to say that her working habits were normal, that other people were lazy. Finally, however, she admitted that she had a deep sense of guilt. Fifteen years earlier, after her father died, she had served as executor of the estate. She had deliberately kept from turning over a large sum of money to her younger brother.

"Why did you do that?" I asked. "Was it a question of greed?"

"Of course not!" she replied. "My brother . . . well, he had a terrible drug problem. I knew what would happen to the money if I turned it over to him. I told myself I was saving it for him, for when he got himself straightened out."

"And . . . ?" I probed.

Harriet took a deep breath. "It never happened. He killed himself. Maybe he didn't do it on purpose, but it came to the same thing. He was only twenty-six. I keep thinking . . . what if I hadn't kept the money? Maybe he would have used it to go into some kind of rehab program. He might still be with us. It's my fault he's dead."

I asked her, "If you had it to do over again, what would you do?"

"I don't know," she said, shaking her head. "But I know I'd try harder to help my brother, instead of being down on him because he had a problem."

"But at the time, did you feel you were justified?" I asked. "Did you feel you were doing the right thing?"

"Sure," she told me. "But now I'm sure it was wrong. That money wasn't mine."

"So you would not do it now?"

"No, I wouldn't," she replied. Her face grew stern. "But that doesn't matter. I can never be forgiven for what I did. I stole from my only brother, and he died. It's only right that God should punish me. I deserve it."

I explained to her that God was not punishing her. She was punishing herself. If you misuse the laws of life, you will suffer accordingly. If you put your hand on a naked charged wire, you will get a shock. The forces of nature are not evil; it is your use of them that determines whether they have a good or evil effect. Electricity is not evil; it depends on whether you use it to light up your home or give someone a fatal shock. The only sin is ignorance of the law, and the only punishment is the automatic reaction of people's misuse of the law.

If you misuse the principles of chemistry, you may blow up your workplace. If you strike your hand against a board, you may cause your hand to bleed. The board is not at fault. The fault lies with your misuse of it.

Eventually I helped Harriet realize that God does not condemn or punish anyone. All her suffering was due to the reaction of her subconscious mind to her own negative and destructive thinking. What she needed was forgiveness, but the true meaning of forgiveness is to forgive yourself. Forgiveness is getting your thoughts in line with the divine law of harmony. Self-condemnation is called *hell* (bondage and restriction); forgiveness is called *heaven* (harmony and peace).

The burden of guilt and self-condemnation was lifted from her mind, and she had a complete healing. The next time she had a checkup, her blood pressure had become normal. The explanation was the cure.

A Murderer Learned to Forgive Himself

Arthur O. murdered a man in Europe many years ago. When he came to me, he was suffering from great mental anguish and torture. He believed that God must punish him for his terrible deed. I asked him what had happened. He explained that he had found out that the other man was having an affair with his wife. He had come upon them unexpectedly, as he returned from hunting, and shot the man in a moment of mad rage. The legal system did not take a very harsh view of his deed; he had to serve only a few months in prison.

When he was released from jail, Arthur divorced his wife and emigrated to the United States. After several years, he met and married an American woman. He and his wife have been

224 The Power of Your Subconscious Mind

blessed with three lovely children. He has made a successful career in a field where he is in a position to help many people. His colleagues like and respect him. None of this seems to help. All this time later, he still blames himself for what he did.

After hearing Arthur's story, I explained to him that scientists tell us every cell of our bodies is replaced every eleven months. Both physically and psychologically, he was no longer the same man who had committed murder, and he had not been for many years. Moreover, he had clearly transformed himself both mentally and spiritually. He was now full of love and goodwill for humanity. The person who committed the crime years before was long since mentally and spiritually dead. In refusing to forgive himself, Arthur was condemning an innocent man.

This explanation had a profound effect upon him. He said it was as if a great weight had been lifted from his mind. He realized for the first time the inner significance of the following truth in the Bible:

> *Come now, let us argue it out, says the Lord. Though your sins are scarlet, they may become white as snow; though they are dyed crimson, they may yet be like wool.* (Isaiah 1:18)

Criticism Cannot Hurt You Without Your Consent

A schoolteacher named Ramona K. came to me after a lecture. She told me that recently she had had to give a speech. Afterward, one of her fellow teachers sent her a note full of criticism. She said that Ramona spoke too fast, swallowed some of her words, and couldn't be heard. Her diction was poor and her text rambled.

Ramona was hurt and angry. She felt deep resentment toward her critic and tried to avoid any contact with her at school.

When I questioned her, Ramona eventually admitted that she deserved many of the criticisms. She was not experienced at speaking to an adult audience. She had been nervous beforehand, and afterward she was simply glad that she had gotten through it. That was the reason she had been so wounded by her coworker's criticisms. It was as if somebody had blasted a toddler for not running fast enough, when simply managing to walk was an amazing feat.

As we talked, Ramona began to see that her first reaction had been childish. She came to agree that the letter was really a blessing and a much-needed corrective. She decided to perfect her lecturing skills by signing up for a course in public speaking at a nearby college. In the meantime, she called up the writer of the note to thank her for her interest and input.

How to Be Compassionate

What if the letter Ramona received was totally incorrect? What if she had good reason to think that the criticisms it made of her speech were simply wrong? In that case, Ramona would have had to realize that something about her speech, whether its manner or its content, had upset the prejudices, superstitions, or narrow sectarian beliefs of the note's writer. The problem would lie not with her but with the writer.

To understand this is to take an essential first step toward compassion. The next logical step would be to pray for the other person's peace, harmony, and understanding. You cannot be hurt when you know that you are master of your thoughts, reactions, and emotions. Emotions follow thoughts, and you have the power to reject all thoughts that may disturb or upset you.

To forgive is to sincerely wish for the other what you wish for yourself: harmony, health, peace, and all the blessings of life.

It is necessary to enter into the spirit of forgiveness and goodwill in order to get good and lasting healing.

Life holds no grudges against you. It is always forgiving you. Life brings you back to health, vitality, harmony, and peace, if you co-operate by thinking in harmony with nature. Negative, hurtful memories, bitterness, and ill will clutter up and impede the free flow of the life-principle within you.

Left at the Altar

Some years ago I was asked to perform a marriage ceremony at a nearby church. The young man did not appear. At the end of two hours, the would-be bride shed a few tears. She then said to me, "I prayed for divine guidance. This may be the answer to my prayer, for 'He never faileth.'"

Her reaction was to restate her faith in God and all things good. She had no bitterness in her heart, because, as she said, "Much as I longed for it, I think this marriage must not have been right action, because my prayer was for right action, not just for me, but for both of us." This young woman sailed serenely through an experience that might have sent another person into an emotional tailspin.

Tune in with the Infinite Intelligence within your subconscious depths. Trust the answer as unquestioningly as you trusted your mother and father when they held you in their arms. This is the high road to poise and mental and emotional health.

It Is Wrong to Marry; Sex Is Evil and I Am Evil

A young woman who heard me speak came up to me afterward. She told me her name was Carol. I was struck by her appearance. She wore a very plain black dress and black stockings.

Her face was pale and bland, without a single touch of lipstick or other makeup. Her manner, too, was subdued yet somehow watchful, as if she imagined that those around her might suddenly start acting in an outrageous way.

Soon Carol was telling me about her upbringing. She was raised by her mother, who taught her to believe that it was a sin to dance, to play cards, to swim, or to go out with men. According to her mother, all men were evil. Sex was nothing but debauchery, inspired by the devil. If she disobeyed these commandments, if she failed to follow them exactly and to the letter, she would burn eternally in hell.

When Carol went out with young men in the office where she worked, she felt a deep sense of guilt. She was convinced that God would punish her. A young man she felt close to asked her to marry him, but she refused. As she said to me, "It is wrong to marry; sex is evil and I am evil." This was her early conditioning speaking.

Of course this young woman felt full of guilt. How could she not? It was impossible for her to live up to her mother's beliefs. It was impossible to avoid the thought that there was something *wrong* with those beliefs. The life-principle that flows through all of us was struggling for recognition and expression.

I suggested to Carol that she try to learn how to forgive herself. To forgive means to give for. She had to give up all these false beliefs for the truths of life and a new estimate of herself.

Carol came to me once weekly for about ten weeks. I taught her what I have learned about the workings of the conscious and subconscious mind, just as I have set it forth in this book. As she gradually came to see that she had been brainwashed, mesmerized, and conditioned by an ignorant, superstitious, bigoted, and frustrated mother, she started to live a wonderful life.

At my suggestion, Carol began to wear more attractive clothes. She visited the cosmetics department of a downtown store for a free comprehensive "makeover." She took dancing lessons and learned to drive. She also learned to swim, to play cards, and to talk with young men. She broke away completely from her family and began to love and value life.

As Carol discovered her inner nature, she began to pray for a companion by claiming that Infinite Spirit would attract to her a man who harmonized with her thoroughly. One evening as she left my office, a man was waiting to see me. I casually introduced them. Six months later, they were married. They are still married and happy with one another.

Forgiveness Is Necessary for Healing

If you have a grievance against anyone, forgive him, so that your Father in heaven may forgive you the wrongs you have done. (Mark 11:25)

Forgiveness of others is essential to mental peace and radiant health. You must forgive everyone who has ever hurt you if you want perfect health and happiness. Forgive yourself by getting your thoughts in harmony with Divine law and order. You cannot forgive yourself completely until you have forgiven others first. To refuse to forgive yourself is nothing more or less than spiritual pride or ignorance.

In the psychosomatic field of medicine today, it is being constantly emphasized that resentment, condemnation of others, remorse, and hostility are behind a host of maladies ranging from arthritis to cardiac disease. The stress caused by these negative emotions can directly affect the immune system of the body, leaving you open to infection and disease.

Specialists in stress-related disorders point out that people who were hurt, mistreated, deceived, or injured often react by filling themselves with resentment and hatred for those who hurt them. This reaction causes inflamed and festering wounds in their subconscious minds. There is only one remedy. They have to cut out and discard their hurts, and the one and only sure way to do this is by forgiveness.

Forgiveness Is Love in Action

The essential ingredient in the art of forgiveness is the willingness to forgive. If you sincerely desire to forgive the other, you are more than halfway over the hurdle. Of course you understand that to forgive another does not necessarily mean that you like that person or want to associate with him or her. You cannot be compelled to like someone. That would be as if the government tried to legislate goodwill, love, peace, or tolerance. You are not going to like a person simply because someone orders you to do so. However—and this is a crucial point—we can love people without liking them.

The Bible says, *Love ye one another.* Impossible as this may sound at first, anyone can do it who really wants to do it. Love means that you wish for the other health, happiness, peace, joy, and all the blessings of life. There is only one prerequisite, and that is sincerity. You are not being magnanimous when you forgive, you are really being selfish, because what you wish for the other, you are actually wishing for yourself. The reason is that you are thinking it and you are feeling it. As you think and feel, so are you. Could anything be simpler than that?

Techniques for Forgiveness

Here is a simple but effective method to bring about forgiveness in yourself. It will work wonders in your life as you practice it. Quiet your mind, relax, and let go. Think of God and his love for you, and then affirm:

I fully and freely forgive [think of the name of the offender]. I release him (her) mentally and spiritually. I completely forgive everything connected with the matter in question. I am free, and he (she) is free. It is a marvelous feeling.

This is my day of general amnesty. I release anybody and everybody who has ever hurt me, and I wish for each and everyone health, happiness, peace, and all the blessings of life. I do this freely, joyously, and lovingly. Whenever I think of the person or persons who hurt me, I say, "I have released you, and all the blessings of life are yours." I am free and they are free. It is wonderful!

The great secret of true forgiveness is that once you have forgiven the person, it is unnecessary to repeat the prayer. Whenever the person comes to your mind, or the particular hurt happens to enter your mind, wish the delinquent well, and say, "Peace be unto you." Do this as often as the thought enters your mind. You will find that after a few days the thought of the person or experience will return less and less often, until it fades into nothingness.

The Acid Test for Forgiveness

Prospectors and jewelers use what is called an acid test to tell if a metal is real gold or an imitation. There is an acid test for forgiveness, too. Imagine that I tell you something wonderful about someone who has wronged you, cheated you, or defrauded you. If you sizzle at hearing the good news about this person, the roots of hatred are still in your subconscious mind, playing havoc with you.

Suppose you had a very painful dental procedure last year and you tell me about it now. If I ask whether you are in pain from it now, you would give me an astonished look and say, "Of course not! I remember the pain, but I don't feel it any longer."

That is the whole story. If you have truly forgiven someone, you will remember the incident, but you will no longer feel the sting or hurt of it. This is the acid test of forgiveness. You must meet it psychologically and spiritually. Otherwise, you are simply deceiving yourself. You are not practicing the true art of forgiveness.

To Understand All Is to Forgive All

Once you understand the creative law of your own mind, you stop blaming other people and conditions for making or marring your life. You realize that your own thoughts and feelings create your destiny. Furthermore, you are aware that externals are not the causes and conditioners of your life and your experiences. To think that others can mar your happiness, that you are the football of a cruel fate, that you must oppose and fight others for a living—all these ideas reveal their destructive nature once you understand that thoughts are things. This principle is clearly set forth in the Bible:

> For as he thinketh in his heart, so is he. (Proverbs 23:7;
> King James)

IDEAS TO REMEMBER

1. God, or life, is no respecter of persons. Life plays no favorites. Life, or God, seems to favor you once you begin to align yourself with the principles of harmony, health, joy, and peace.

2. God, or life, never sends disease, sickness, accident, or suffering. We bring these things on ourselves by our own negative destructive thinking, based upon the law *As we sow, so shall we reap.*

3. Your concept of God is the most important thing in your life. If you really believe in a God of love, your subconscious mind will respond by bringing countless blessings to you. Believe in a God of love.

4. Life, or God, holds no grudge against you. Life never condemns you. Life heals a cut on your hand. Life forgives you if you burn your finger. It reduces the edema and restores the part to wholeness and perfection.

5. Your guilt complex is a false concept of God and life. God, or life, does not punish or judge you. You do this to yourself by the subconscious effects of your false beliefs, negative thinking, and self-condemnation.

6. God, or life, does not condemn or punish you. The forces of nature are not evil. The effect of their use depends on how you use the power within you. You can use electricity to kill someone or to light the house. You can use water to drown a child or quench his thirst. Good and evil come right back to the thought and purpose in a person's own mind.

7. God, or life, never punishes. People punish themselves by their false concepts of God, life, and the universe. Their thoughts are creative, and they create their own misery.

8. If another criticizes you, and these faults are within you, rejoice, give thanks, and appreciate the comments. This gives you the opportunity to correct the particular fault.

9. You cannot be hurt by criticism when you know that you are master of your thoughts, reactions, and emotions. This gives you the opportunity to pray for and bless the other, thereby blessing yourself.

10. When you pray for guidance and right action, take what comes. Realize it is good and very good. Then there is no cause for self-pity, criticism, or hatred.

11. There is nothing good or bad, but thinking makes it so. There is no evil in the desire for food, sex, wealth, or true expression. It depends on how you use these urges, desires, or aspirations. Your desire for food can be met without killing someone for a loaf of bread.

12. Resentment, hatred, ill will, and hostility are behind a host of maladies. Forgive yourself and everybody else by pouring out love, life, joy, and goodwill to all who have hurt you. Continue until such time as you can meet them in your mind and know that you are at peace with them.

13. To forgive is to give something for. Give love, peace, joy, wisdom, and all the blessings of life to the other, until there is no sting left in your mind. This is the acid test of forgiveness.

14. If someone has hurt you, lied about and vilified you, and has said all manner of evil about you, is your thought of that person negative? If so, you have not yet forgiven. The roots of hatred are still in your subconscious mind, playing havoc with you and your good. The only way to wither those roots is with love. Wish for the person all the blessings of life. This is the meaning of *Forgive until seventy times seven.*

Forgiveness of others is essential to mental peace and radiant health. You must forgive everyone who has ever hurt you if you want perfect health and happiness. Forgive yourself by getting your thoughts in harmony with Divine law and order. You cannot forgive yourself completely until you have forgiven others first. To refuse to forgive yourself is nothing more or less than spiritual pride or ignorance.

Chapter Eighteen

How Your Subconscious Mind Removes Mental Blocks

You can build the idea of freedom and peace of mind into your mentality so that it reaches your subconscious depths. The latter, being all-powerful, will free you from all desire to follow your bad habit. At that point, you will achieve a new understanding of how your mind works. You will discover within yourself the infinite resources to back up your statement and prove the truth to yourself.

What can you do if you are faced with a difficult situation and you cannot see your way clear? The solution lies within the problem. Every question implies its own answer. The Infinite Intelligence within your subconscious mind knows all and sees all. It has the answer and is revealing it to you now . . . but you must *listen*. You must follow the urgings of your subconscious mind with perfect confidence. Once you achieve this new mental attitude—that the creative intelligence within you is bringing about a happy solution—you will find the answer you seek. Rest assured that such an attitude of mind will bring order, peace, and meaning to all your undertakings.

How to Break or Build a Habit

We are all creatures of habit. Habit is a function of our subconscious minds. We learned to swim, ride a bicycle, dance, and drive a car by consciously doing these things over and over again until they established tracks in our subconscious minds. Then, the automatic habit action of the subconscious mind took over. This is sometimes referred to as "second nature," that is, the reaction of the subconscious mind to the thinking and acting that makes up our "first" nature.

If we create our own habits, it follows that we are free to *choose* good habits or bad habits. If you repeat a negative thought or act over a period of time, you will place yourself under the compulsion of a habit. The law of your subconscious is compulsion.

Breaking the Habit of Drink

When Bob J. came to me, he was close to despair. "I've lost my job, my wife, and my family to drink," he told me. "My wife won't even speak to me on the phone. She won't let me see our daughter. I don't know where to turn."

"Have you tried to stop drinking?" I asked.

"Of course I have," he said. "Lots of times. And I have stopped, too, for a little while. Then I get an uncontrollable urge, and the next thing I know, I'm coming off a two-week bender. It's terrible!"

Time and again these experiences had occurred to this unfortunate man. He realized that binge drinking had become a habit, and he saw that he had to change the habit and establish a new one. However, his continued efforts to suppress his cravings made matters only worse. His repeated failures convinced him that he was hopeless and powerless to control his urge or obsession. This idea of being powerless operated as a tremendous suggestion to his subconscious mind and aggravated his weakness, making his life a succession of failures.

I taught him to harmonize the functions of the conscious and subconscious mind. When these two cooperate, the idea or desire implanted in the subconscious mind is realized. His reasoning mind agreed that if the old habit path or track had carried him into trouble, he could consciously form a new path to freedom, sobriety, and peace of mind.

He knew that while his destructive habit had become automatic, he had acquired it through his conscious choice. He realized that if he had been conditioned negatively, he also could be conditioned positively. As a result, he stopped thinking that he was powerless to overcome the habit. He achieved a clear understanding that there was no obstacle to his healing other than his own thought. Therefore, there was no occasion for great mental effort or mental coercion.

The Power of a Mental Picture

Bob began to make a practice of relaxing his body and getting into a drowsy, meditative state. Then he filled his mind with the picture of the desired end, knowing his subconscious mind could bring it about the easiest way. He imagined his daughter giving him a welcoming hug and saying, "Oh, Daddy, it's so wonderful to have you home again!"

Regularly, systematically, he sat down and meditated in this way. When his attention wandered, he made it a habit to immediately recall the mental picture of his daughter with her smile and the scene of his home enlivened by her cheerful voice. All this brought about a reconditioning of his mind. It was a gradual process. He kept it up. He persevered, knowing that sooner or later he would establish a new habit pattern in his subconscious mind.

I told him that he could liken his conscious mind to a camera, that his subconscious mind was the sensitive plate on which he registered and impressed the picture. This made a profound impression on him. His whole aim became to firmly impress the picture on his mind and develop it there. Films are developed in the dark; likewise, mental pictures are developed in the darkroom of the subconscious mind.

Focused Attention

Bob understood that his conscious mind was like a camera, so he used no effort. There was no mental struggle. He quietly adjusted his thoughts and focused his attention on the scene before him until he gradually identified with the picture. He became absorbed in the mental atmosphere, repeating the mental movie frequently.

There was no room for doubt that a healing would follow. When there was any temptation to drink, he would switch his imagination from any thoughts of drinking bouts to the feeling of being at home with his family. He was successful because he confidently expected to experience the picture he was developing in his mind. Today he is sober, reunited with his family, successful in his career, and radiantly happy.

Jinxed

"For the last three months, I've been running into one roadblock after another. I really think I've got a jinx following me!"

Ruth B. was the founder of a firm that handles billing and record-keeping for professionals. Her company was very successful at first, but then something changed.

"I don't get it," she told me. "Suddenly it's as if all the doors that were opening to me are jammed shut. Time after time, I bring potential clients right to the point of signing on the dotted line. Then, at the eleventh hour, they back out. What's going on?"

"How long have you had this problem?" I asked.

"Like I said, about three months," she replied. "Since the middle of April."

Curious, I asked, "What makes you so sure about the date? Did anything in particular happen then?"

She scowled. "You better believe it! I was making a pitch to a certain orthodontist. I'm not going to say his name, but if your kid has braces, you probably know him. I laid it all out. I showed him how much time and effort and money he'd save if my outfit handled all his clerical scut work. He saw the sense of it and made a verbal commitment. But when I mailed him the contract, first he stalled and then he backed out. I was fit to be tied!"

"And after that . . . ?" I probed.

"It started happening over and over," Ruth said. For a moment she covered her eyes. "I'm jinxed! There's no other explanation."

"Yes, there is," I told her. I explained that her irritation and resentment toward the orthodontist had given her a subconscious belief that other prospective clients would also back out on her. This belief set up a pattern of frustration, hostility, and obstacles. She gradually built up in her mind an expectation of last-minute cancellations. Once this was impressed upon her subconscious mind, it began to bring about the conditions she dreaded. And each successive failure strengthened the conviction that she was doomed to fail. She had established a vicious circle.

As we continued to talk, Ruth began to see that the trouble was in her own mind. She realized that the cure was to change her mental attitude. She began to meditate in this manner:

I realize I am one with the Infinite Intelligence of my subconscious mind, which knows no obstacle, difficulty, or delay. I live in the joyous expectancy of the best. My deeper mind responds to my thoughts. I know that the work of the Infinite Power of my subconscious cannot be hindered. Infinite Intelligence always finishes successfully whatever it begins.

Creative wisdom works through me bringing all my plans and purposes to completion. Whatever I start, I bring to a successful conclusion. My aim in life is to give wonderful service, and all those whom I contact are blessed by what I have to offer. All my work comes to full fruition in Divine order.

She repeated this prayer every morning before going to call on her customers. She also prayed each night before going to sleep. In a short time she had established a new habit pattern in her subconscious mind. Soon she was once again successful in convincing prospective clients to sign up with her company. All thought of being the victim of a jinx was forgotten.

How Much Do You Want What You Want?

The story is told that a young man asked Socrates how he could get wisdom.

"Come with me," Socrates replied. He took the lad to a river and shoved his head underwater. He held it there until the boy struggled for air. Then he let him go.

Once the boy regained his composure, Socrates asked him, "What did you desire most when your head was underwater?"

"I wanted air," the boy told him.

Socrates nodded slowly. "When you want wisdom as much as you wanted air when you were immersed in the water," he said, "you will receive it."

In the same way, when

- you have an intense, sincere desire to overcome a certain block in your life;

- you come to a clear-cut decision that there is a way out;

- you confidently decide that that is the course you wish to follow,

then victory and triumph are assured.

If you really want peace of mind and inner calm, you will get it. It doesn't matter how unjustly you have been treated, or how unfair the boss has been, or what a mean scoundrel someone has proved to be. All this makes no difference to you when you awaken to your mental and spiritual powers. You know what you want, and you will definitely refuse to let the thieves (thoughts) of hatred, anger, hostility, and ill will rob you of peace, harmony, health, and happiness.

Once you learn the habit of identifying your thoughts immediately with your aim in life, you cease to become upset by people, conditions, news, and events. Your aim is peace, health, inspiration, harmony, and abundance. Feel a river of peace flowing through you now. Your thought is the immaterial and invisible power, and you choose to let it bless, inspire, and give you peace.

If you have a keen desire to free yourself from any destructive habit, you are already 51 percent healed. When your desire to give up the bad habit is greater than your need to continue it, you will be amazed to discover that complete freedom is but a step away.

If you are seeking promotion in your work, imagine your employer, supervisor, or loved one congratulating you on your promotion.

*Make the picture vivid and real. Hear the voice, see the gestures,
and feel the reality of it all. Continue to do this frequently and you
will experience the joy of the answered prayer.*

Why He Could Not Be Healed

Allan S. was a field representative for a major textbook distributor. He was married, with four children, but he was also involved in a secret relationship with another woman during his business trips. When he came to see me, he was nervous and irritable. He could not get to sleep without pills. He had high blood pressure and an assortment of internal pains that his doctor could not diagnose or relieve. To make matters worse, he was drinking heavily.

As we quickly discovered, the cause of all this was a deep unconscious sense of guilt. The religious creed he had been brought up in was deeply lodged in his subconscious mind. It placed great stress on the sanctity of the marriage vows, yet he was violating them flagrantly and constantly. He drank to excess in a vain attempt to heal the wound of guilt. Just as an invalid might take morphine and codeine for severe pains, he was taking alcohol for the pain or wound in his mind. It was the old story of adding fuel to the fire.

The Explanation and the Cure

He listened to my explanation of how his mind worked. He faced his problem, considered it carefully, and made a decision to give up his illicit relationship. He also realized that his drinking was an unconscious attempt to escape. The hidden cause lodged in his subconscious mind had to be eradicated. Only then would healing follow.

He began to impress his subconscious mind three times a day, using this prayer:

My mind is full of peace, poise, balance, and equilibrium. The infinite lies stretched in smiling repose within me. I am not afraid of anything in the past, the present, or the future. The Infinite Intelligence of my subconscious mind leads, guides, and directs me in all ways.

I now meet every situation with faith, poise, calmness, and confidence. I am now completely free from the habit. My mind is full of inner peace, freedom, and joy. I forgive myself; then I am forgiven. Peace, sobriety, and confidence reign supreme in my mind.

As he repeated this prayer, he was fully aware of what he was doing and why he was doing it. Knowing what he was doing gave him necessary faith and confidence. I explained to him that as he spoke these statements out loud, slowly, lovingly, and meaningfully, they would gradually sink into his subconscious mind. Like seeds, they would grow after their kind. His ears heard the sound, and the healing vibrations of the words reached his subconscious mind and obliterated all the negative mental patterns that had caused his problems. Light dispels darkness. The constructive thought destroys the negative thought. He became a transformed man within a month.

Refusing to Admit a Bad Habit

If you are an alcoholic or drug addict, admit it. Do not dodge the issue. Many people remain alcoholics because they refuse to admit it.

Your disease is an instability, an inner fear. You are refusing to face life, and so you try to escape your responsibilities through the bottle. As an alcoholic you have no free will. You may think you have. You may even boast about your willpower.

If you are a habitual drunkard and you assert boldly, "I will not touch it anymore," you do not have the power to make this assertion come true. The reason is that you do not know where to *locate* the power.

You are living in a psychological prison of your own making. You are bound by your beliefs, opinions, training, and environmental influences. Like most people, you are a creature of habit. You are conditioned to react the way you do.

Building the Idea of Freedom

You can build the idea of freedom and peace of mind into your mentality so that it reaches your subconscious depths. The latter, being all-powerful, will free you from all desire for alcohol. At that point, you will achieve a new understanding of how your mind works. You will discover within yourself the infinite resources to back up your statement and prove the truth to yourself.

Fifty-one Percent Healed

If you have a keen desire to free yourself from any destructive habit, you are already 51 percent healed. When your desire to give up the bad habit is greater than your need to continue it, you will be amazed to discover that complete freedom is but a step away.

Whatever thought you anchor the mind upon, the mind magnifies. Engage the mind on the concept of freedom (that is, freedom from the destructive habit) and peace of mind. Keep it focused on this new direction of attention. In doing so, you generate feelings that gradually pervade the concept of freedom and peace. Whatever idea you emotionalize in this way is accepted by your subconscious and brought to pass.

The Law of Substitution

Realize that something good can come out of your suffering. You have not suffered in vain. However, it is foolish to continue to suffer.

If you continue as an alcoholic, it will bring about mental and physical deterioration and decay. Realize that the power in your subconscious is backing you up. Even though you may be seized with melancholia, you can begin to imagine the joy of freedom that is in store for you.

This is the law of substitution. Your imagination took you to the bottle. Let it now take you to freedom and peace of mind. You will suffer a little, but it is for a constructive purpose. You will bear it like a mother in the pangs of childbirth, and you will bring forth a child of the mind. Your subconscious will give birth to sobriety.

The Cause of Alcoholism

The real cause of alcoholism is negative and destructive thinking; for *as humans think, so are they*. The alcoholic has a deep sense of inferiority, inadequacy, frustration, and defeat. Often these are accompanied by a deep inner hostility. He or she has countless alibis to explain his or her drinking, but in reality the sole reason is in the person's *thought life*.

Three Magic Steps

The first step: Get still; quiet the wheels of the mind. Enter into a sleepy, drowsy state. In this relaxed, peaceful, receptive state, you are preparing for the second step.

The second step: Take a brief phrase that can be graven readily on the memory and repeat it over and over as a lullaby. Use the phrase "Sobriety and peace of mind are mine now, and

I give thanks." To prevent the mind from wandering, repeat it aloud or sketch its pronunciation with the lips and tongue as you say it mentally. This helps its entry into the subconscious mind. Do this for five minutes or more. You will find a deep emotional response.

The third step: Just before going to sleep, practice what Johann von Goethe, the great German poet, used to do. Imagine a friend or loved one with you. Your eyes are closed, you are relaxed and at peace. The loved one or friend is subjectively present, and is saying to you, "Congratulations!"

You see the smile; you hear the voice. You mentally touch the hand; all is real and vivid. The word *congratulations* implies complete freedom. Hear it over and over until you get the subconscious reaction that satisfies.

Perseverance

When fear knocks at the door of your mind, or when worry, anxiety, and doubt cross your mind, behold your vision, your goal. Think of the Infinite Power within your subconscious mind, which can generate your thinking and imagining. This will give you confidence, power, and courage. Keep on, persevere, *until the day breaks, and the shadows flee away.*

IDEAS TO REMEMBER

1. The solution lies within the problem. The answer is in every question. Infinite Intelligence responds to you as you call upon it with faith and confidence.

2. Habit is the function of your subconscious mind. There is no greater evidence of the marvelous power of your subconscious than the force and sway habit holds in your life. You are a creature of habit.

3. You form habit patterns in your subconscious mind by repeating a thought or act over and over until it establishes tracks in the subconscious mind and becomes automatic.

4. You have freedom to choose. You can choose a good habit or a bad habit. Prayer or meditation is a good habit.

5. Whatever mental picture, backed by faith, you behold in your conscious mind, your subconscious mind will bring to pass.

6. The only obstacle to your success and achievement is your own thought or mental image.

7. When your attention wanders, bring it back to the contemplation of your good or goal. Make a habit of this. This is called disciplining the mind.

8. Your conscious mind is the camera, and your subconscious mind is the sensitive plate on which you register or impress the picture.

9. The only jinx that follows anyone is a fear thought repeated over and over in the mind. Break the jinx by knowing that whatever you start you will bring to a conclusion in Divine order. Picture the happy ending and sustain it with confidence.

10. To form a new habit, you must be convinced that it is desirable. When your desire to give up the bad habit is greater than your desire to continue, you are already 51 percent healed.

11. The statements of others cannot hurt you except through your own thoughts and mental participation. Identify yourself with your aim, which is peace, harmony, and joy. You are the only thinker in your universe.

12. Excessive drinking is an unconscious desire to escape. The cause of alcoholism is negative and destructive thinking. The cure is to think of freedom, sobriety, and perfection and to feel the thrill of accomplishment.

13. Many people remain alcoholics because they refuse to admit their problem.

14. The law of your subconscious mind, which held you in bondage and inhibited your freedom of action, will give you freedom and happiness. It depends on how you use it.

15. Your imagination took you to the bottle; let it take you to freedom by imagining you are free.

16. The real cause of alcoholism is negative and destructive thinking. *As a man thinks in his heart* [subconscious mind], *so is he.*

17. When fear knocks at the door of your mind, let faith in God and all things good open the door.

If you have an intense, sincere desire to overcome a certain block in your life; if you come to a clear-cut decision that there is a way out; if you confidently decide that that is the course you wish to follow, then victory and triumph are assured.

Chapter Nineteen

How to Use Your Subconscious Mind to Remove Fear

It has been said that a person's greatest enemy is fear. Fear is behind failure, sickness, and poor human relations. Millions of people are afraid of the past, the future, old age, insanity, and death. But fear is a thought in your mind. This means that you are afraid of your own thoughts.

One of my students was invited to speak at the annual banquet of his professional association. He told me he was panic-stricken at the thought of speaking before a thousand people, many of whom were influential in his field. He overcame his fear this way: For several nights he sat calmly in an armchair for about five minutes. He said to himself slowly, quietly, and positively:

I am going to master this fear. I am overcoming it now. I speak with poise and confidence. I am relaxed and at ease.

In this way, he set into operation a definite law of mind. When the time came, he overcame his fear and gave a very successful speech.

The subconscious mind is amenable to suggestion. It is *controlled* by suggestion. When you still your mind and relax, the thoughts of your conscious mind sink into the subconscious. The process is similar to osmosis, in which fluids separated by a porous membrane intermingle. As these positive seeds, or thoughts, sink into the subconscious area, they grow after their kind, and you become poised, serene, and calm.

Our Greatest Enemy

It has been said that a person's greatest enemy is fear. Fear is behind failure, sickness, and poor human relations. Millions of people are afraid of the past, the future, old age, insanity, and death. But fear is a thought in your mind. This means that you are afraid of your own thoughts.

A small child can be paralyzed with fear when a playmate says there is a monster under the bed who will grab him in the night. But when the parent turns on the light and shows there is no monster, he is freed from fear. The fear in the mind of the child was every bit as real as if there were really a monster there. He was healed of a false thought in his mind. The thing he feared did not exist. In the same way, most of your fears have no reality. They are merely a conglomeration of sinister shadows, and shadows have no reality.

Do the Thing You Fear

Ralph Waldo Emerson, the great nineteenth-century philosopher and poet, said, "Do the thing you are afraid to do, and the death of fear is certain."

There was a time when I was filled with unutterable fear at the thought of standing before an audience and speaking. If I had given way to this fear, terrible as it was, I am sure you would not now be reading this book. I would never have been able to share with others what I have learned about the workings of the subconscious mind.

The way I overcame this fear was to follow Emerson's advice. Quaking inside, I went before audiences and spoke. Gradually I became less fearful, until at last I was comfortable enough to enjoy what I was doing. I even grew to look forward to speaking engagements. I did the thing I was afraid to do, and the death of fear was certain.

When you affirm positively that you are going to master your fears, and you come to a definite decision in your conscious mind, you release the power of the subconscious, which flows in response to the nature of your thought.

Banishing Stage Fright

Judy L., a suburban Pennsylvania wife and mother, was proud of her expertise in painting floral scenes on china. Many of her friends displayed her art in their homes. When her daughter's teacher asked her to come to the class and talk about her hobby, she declined because of her great fear of speaking in public—even to a class of eight-year-olds. She had read in my books my suggestions on overcoming fear and determined to follow them.

Every morning when she awoke and every evening before she went to sleep, she'd relax and repeat this meditation:

> I am a talented artist and I can share my skills so others can appreciate and even learn them. I am not afraid to talk to groups about it. I will speak to my daughter's class and then to other groups.

After a few months, she went to the school and showed the children some of her work and explained how she did it. She wrote to me that not only did the children and the teacher thank her, but other teachers asked her to speak to their classes. From that time on, Judy lost all fear of speaking in public and later joined the Toastmasters Club, a group of men and women who meet regularly to give talks and improve their public speaking confidence and ability.

If you adapt this procedure to your situation and carry it out sincerely and confidently, the death of fear is certain.

Fear of Failure

I often get visits from students at a nearby university. One complaint many of them share is what we can call suggestive amnesia during examinations. They all tell me the same thing: "I know the material cold before the exam, and I remember all the answers after the exam. But when I'm in the classroom staring down at a blank exam booklet, my mind goes totally blank!"

A great many of us have had similar experiences. The explanation lies in one of the major laws of the subconscious mind. The idea that realizes itself is the one to which we give the most concentrated attention. In talking with these students, I find that they are most attentive to the idea of failure. As a result, it is failure that the subconscious mind brings into reality. The fear of failure itself creates the experience of failure, by way of a temporary amnesia.

A medical student named Sheila A. was one of the most brilliant students in her class. Yet when she faced a written or oral examination, she found herself going blank at even simple questions. I explained the reason to her. She had been worrying and brooding over the chances of failure for several days before the exam. These negative thoughts became charged with fear.

Thoughts enveloped in the powerful emotion of fear are realized in the subconscious mind. In other words, this young student was requesting her subconscious mind to see to it that she failed, and that is exactly what it did.

As Sheila studied the working of her subconscious mind, she learned that it is the storehouse of memory. It had a perfect record of everything she had heard and read during her medical training. Moreover, she learned that the subconscious mind is responsive and reciprocal. The way to be in deep rapport with it is to be relaxed, peaceful, and confident.

Every night and morning, she began to imagine her parents congratulating her on her wonderful record. She would hold an imaginary letter from them in her hand. As she began to contemplate this happy result, she called forth a corresponding or reciprocal response or reaction in herself.

Under this consistent stimulation, the all-wise and omnipotent power of the subconscious took over. It dictated and directed her conscious mind accordingly. She imagined the end, thereby willing the means to the realization of the end. After following this procedure, she had no trouble passing her subsequent exams. The subjective wisdom of her subconscious mind took over and *compelled* her to give an excellent account of herself.

Fear of Water

When I was about ten years old, I accidentally fell into a swimming pool. I had never learned to swim. I flailed my arms, but it did no good. I felt myself sinking. I can still remember the terror as the dark water surrounded me. I tried to gasp for air, but my mouth filled with water. At the last moment, another boy noticed my plight. He jumped in and pulled me out. This experience sank into my subconscious mind. The result was that for years I feared the water.

Then one day I mentioned this irrational fear of mine to a wise elderly psychologist.

"Go down to the swimming pool," he told me. "Look at the water. It is simply a chemical compound, made up of two atoms of hydrogen and one of oxygen. It has no will, no awareness. But you have *both*."

I nodded, wondering where this was leading.

"Once you understand that the water is essentially passive," he continued, "say out loud in a strong voice, 'I am going to master you. By the powers of mind, I will dominate you.' Then go into the water. Take swimming lessons. Use your inner powers to overcome the water."

I did as I was told. Once I assumed a new attitude of mind, the omnipotent power of the subconscious responded, giving me strength, faith, and confidence. It enabled me to overcome my fear, and I mastered the water. Today I swim every morning for both health and pleasure. Do not permit water to master you. Remember, you are the master of the water.

A Master Technique for Overcoming Fear

Here is a technique for overcoming fear that I have taught from the lecture platform to thousands of people. It works like a charm. Try it!

Suppose you are afraid of swimming. Begin now to sit still for five or ten minutes three or four times a day. Put yourself into a state of deep relaxation. Now imagine you are swimming. Subjectively, you *are* swimming. Mentally you have projected yourself into the water. You feel the brisk coolness of the water and the movement of your arms and legs. It is all real, vivid, and a joyous activity of the mind.

This is not idle daydreaming. You understand that what you are experiencing in your imagination will be developed in your subconscious mind. Then you will be compelled to express the image and likeness of the picture you impressed on your deeper mind. When you next attempt to swim, it is the joy that will surface. This is the law of the subconscious.

You can apply the same technique to other fears. If you are afraid of high places, imagine you are taking a stroll in the mountains. Feel the reality of it all. Enjoy the pure air, the alpine flowers, the thrilling scenery. Know that as you continue to do this mentally, you will come to do it physically with ease and comfort.

He Blessed the Elevator

Jonathan M. is an executive with a large corporation. For many years he was terrified to ride in an elevator. He would walk up seven flights of stairs to his office every morning to avoid the elevator ride. When he had to meet with people from other companies whose offices were on high floors, he always found some excuse to meet them at his own office or at a restaurant. Business trips out of town were torture for him. He had to call ahead, to make sure his hotel room was on a low floor and that he would be able to use the stairs.

This fear was the product of his subconscious mind, perhaps in response to some experience that he had long since forgotten on a conscious level. Once he learned this, he set about to change it. He began to bless the elevator every night and several times a day. In a calm, confident mood, he repeated to himself:

> The elevator in our building is a wonderful idea. It came out of the universal mind. It is a boon and a blessing to all our employees. It gives wonderful service. It operates in Divine order. I ride in it in peace and joy. I remain silent now while the currents of life, love, and understanding flow through the patterns of my thought.

In my imagination I am now in the elevator, and I step out into my office. The elevator is full of our employees. I talk to them, and they are friendly, joyous, and free. It is a wonderful experience of freedom, faith, and confidence. I give thanks.

He continued this prayer for ten days. On the eleventh day, he walked into the elevator with other members of his company and felt completely free.

The subconscious mind is amenable to suggestion. It is controlled by suggestion. When you still your mind and relax, the thoughts of your conscious mind sink into the subconscious. The process is similar to osmosis, in which fluids separated by a porous membrane intermingle. As these positive seeds, or thoughts, sink into the subconscious area, they grow after their kind, and you become poised, serene, and calm.

When faced with an abnormal fear, place your attention on the thing immediately desired. Get absorbed and engrossed in your desire. Know that the subjective always overturns the objective. This attitude will give you confidence and lift your spirits. The Infinite Power of your subconscious mind is moving on your behalf. It cannot fail. Therefore, peace and assurance are yours.

When fear knocks at the door of your mind, or when worry, anxiety, and doubt cross your mind, behold your vision, your goal. Think of the Infinite Power within your subconscious mind, which can generate your thinking and imagining. This will give you confidence, power, and courage. Keep on, persevere, until the day breaks, and the shadows flee away.

Normal Fear

A newborn baby has only two basic fears, the fear of falling and the fear of sudden loud noises. These are perfectly normal. They serve as a sort of alarm system given you by nature as a means of self-preservation.

Normal fear is good. You hear an automobile coming down the road toward you and you step aside to survive. The momentary fear of being run over is overcome by your action.

All other fears are abnormal. They were caused by particular experiences or were passed along to you by parents, relatives, teachers, and others who influenced your early years.

Abnormal Fear

Abnormal fear takes hold when people let their imagination run riot. I knew a woman who was invited to go on a trip around the world by plane. She began to cut out of the newspapers all reports of airplane catastrophes. She even ordered a videotape of *The World's Worst Airplane Crashes.* She imagined herself going down in the ocean and drowning. This is abnormal fear. Had she persisted in this, there is a strong chance that she would have attracted to herself what she feared most.

Another example of someone who suffered from abnormal fear is a businessman in New York who was very successful and prosperous. He created his own private mental motion picture in which his company was forced into bankruptcy and he lost everything. The more he ran this mental movie of failure, the more he sank into a deep depression. He refused to stop this morbid imagery. He kept telling his wife, "This can't last"; "The boom will end any day now"; "It's all hopeless; we're going to go broke."

His wife later told me that in the end he did go bankrupt. All the things he imagined and feared came to pass. The things he feared did not exist, but he brought them to pass by constantly fearing, believing, and expecting financial disaster. As Job said, *The thing I feared has come upon me.*

The world is full of people who are afraid that something terrible will happen to their children or that some dread catastrophe will befall them. When they read about an epidemic of some rare disease, they live in fear that they will catch it. Some imagine they have the disease already. All this is abnormal fear.

The Answer to Abnormal Fear

If you find yourself beset with an abnormal fear, you must strive to move mentally to the opposite. If you remain at the extreme of fear, you will suffer stagnation plus mental and physical deterioration. When fear arises, one of the basic laws of the subconscious mind immediately brings with it a desire for something opposite to the thing feared.

Place your attention on the thing immediately desired. Get absorbed and engrossed in your desire. Know that the subjective always overturns the objective. This attitude will give you confidence and lift your spirits. The Infinite Power of your subconscious mind is moving on your behalf. It cannot fail. Therefore, peace and assurance are yours.

Examine Your Fears

The head of sales for a major multinational corporation confided that when he first began working as a salesperson, he had to walk around the block five or six times before he could get up the nerve to call on a customer.

His supervisor was both very experienced and very perceptive. One day she said to him, "Don't be afraid of the monster hiding behind the door. There is no monster. You are the victim of a false belief."

The supervisor went on to tell him that whenever she felt the first stirrings of a fear, she stood up to it. She stared it in the face, looking it straight in the eye. When she did that, she always found that her fear faded and shrank into insignificance.

Out of the Jungle of Fear

A former U.S. Army chaplain named John N. told me that during World War II, the plane he was in was hit and damaged by anti-aircraft fire. He had to bail out over the jungle-clad mountains of New Guinea. Of course he was frightened, but he knew that fear came in two varieties, normal and abnormal. The abnormal kind, which was trying to take control of him, was a close relative of panic.

He decided to do something about his fear immediately. He began to talk to himself, saying, "John, you can't surrender to your fear. Your fear is a desire for safety and security, and a way out."

He stood in the center of a small clearing and calmed his breathing. He pushed away the first symptoms of panic. As soon as he felt more relaxed, he began to claim, "Infinite Intelligence, which guides the planets in their courses, is now leading and guiding me out of this jungle to safety." He kept saying this out loud to himself for ten minutes or more.

"Suddenly," John told me, "I felt something start to stir inside me. It was a mood of confidence and faith. I was drawn to one side of the clearing. There I found the faint trace of a path, and I began to walk. Two days later, I miraculously came upon a small village where the people were friendly. They fed me, then took me to the edge of the jungle, where a rescue plane picked me up."

John's changed mental attitude saved him. His confidence and trust in the subjective wisdom and power within him gave him the solution to his problem.

He added, "If I had started to bemoan my fate and indulge my fears, the monster fear would have conquered me. I probably would have died of fear and starvation."

He Fired Himself

Rafael S. was an executive in a major foundation. He admitted to me that for three years he had been terrified he would lose his position. He was always imagining failure. He kept expecting his subordinates to be promoted over his head. The thing he feared did not exist, save as a morbid anxious thought in his own mind. His vivid imagination dramatized the loss of his job until he became increasingly nervous and inefficient. Finally he was asked to resign.

In reality, Rafael dismissed himself. His constant negative imagery, the flood of fear suggestions he sent to his subconscious mind, caused the subconscious mind to respond and react accordingly. It led him to make mistakes and foolish decisions. These in turn created his failure. He might never have been fired if he had immediately moved to the opposite in his mind.

They Plotted Against Him

During a world lecture tour, I had a two-hour conversation with a prominent government official in one of the countries I visited. I found that this man had a deep sense of inner peace and serenity. He said that although he is constantly showered with abuse by newspapers that support the opposition party, he never allows it to disturb him. His practice is to sit still for fifteen minutes in the morning and realize that in the center of himself is a deep, still ocean of peace. Meditating in this way, he generates tremendous power, which overcomes all manner of difficulties and fears.

A few months earlier, he had received a midnight call from a panicky colleague. According to his coworker, a group of people were plotting against him. They intended to overthrow his administration by force, with help from dissident elements of the country's armed forces.

In reply, the official told his colleague, "I am going to sleep now in perfect peace. We can discuss this tomorrow at 10:00 a.m."

As he explained to me, "I know that no negative thought can ever manifest itself unless I emotionalize the thought and accept it mentally. I refuse to entertain their suggestion of fear. Therefore, no harm can come to me unless I allow it."

Notice how calm he was, how cool, how serene! He did not get overwrought and start tearing his hair or wringing his hands. At his center he found the still water, an inner peace, and there was a great calm.

Deliver Yourself from All Your Fears

In the Bible there is a perfect formula for casting out fear:

> *I sought the Lord's help and he answered me; he set me free from all my terrors.* (Psalm 34:4)

Lord is an ancient word meaning *law*—the power of your subconscious mind.

Learn the wonders of your subconscious. Understand how it works and functions. Master the techniques given to you in this chapter. Put them into practice now, today! Your subconscious will respond, and you will be free of all fears

IDEAS TO REMEMBER

1. Do the thing you are afraid to do, and the death of fear is certain. If you say to yourself with perfect confidence and faith, "I am going to master this fear," you will.

2. Fear is a negative thought in your mind. Supplant it with a constructive thought. Fear has killed millions.

Confidence is greater than fear. Nothing is more powerful than faith in God and the good.

3. Fear is a person's greatest enemy. It is behind failure, sickness, and bad human relations. Love casts out fear. Love is an emotional attachment to the good things of life. Fall in love with honesty, integrity, justice, goodwill, and success. Live in the joyous expectancy of the best, and invariably the best will come to you.

4. Counteract fear suggestions with the opposite, such as, "I sing beautifully; I am poised, serene, and calm." It will pay fabulous dividends.

5. Fear is behind the suggestive amnesia that strikes during examinations. You can overcome this by affirming frequently, "I have a perfect memory for everything I need to know." Imagine a friend congratulating you on your brilliant success on the exam. Persevere and you will win.

6. If you are afraid to cross water, swim. In your imagination swim freely, joyously. Project yourself into the water mentally. Feel the chill and thrill of swimming across the pool. Make it vivid. As you do this subjectively, you will be compelled to go into the water and conquer it. This is the law of your mind.

7. If you are afraid of closed places, such as elevators, mentally ride in an elevator while sincerely blessing all its parts and functions. You will be amazed how quickly the fear will be dissipated.

8. You were born with only two fears, the fear of falling and the fear of noise. All your other fears were acquired. Get rid of them.

9. Normal fear is good. Abnormal fear is very bad and destructive. To constantly indulge in fear thoughts results in abnormal fear, obsessions, and complexes. To fear something persistently causes a sense of panic and terror.

10. You can overcome abnormal fear when you know the power of your subconscious mind can change conditions and bring to pass the cherished desires of your heart. Give your immediate attention and devotion to your desire, which is the opposite of your fear. This is the love that casts out fear.

11. If you are afraid of failure, give attention to success. If you are afraid of sickness, dwell on perfect health. If you are afraid of an accident, dwell on the guidance and protection of God. If you are afraid of death, dwell on eternal life. God is life, and that is your life now.

12. The great law of substitution is the answer to fear. Whatever you fear has its solution in the form of your desire. If you are sick, you desire health. If you are in the prison of fear, you desire freedom. Expect the good. Mentally concentrate on the good, and know that your subconscious mind answers you always. It never fails.

13. The things you fear do not really exist except as thoughts in your mind. Thoughts are creative. This is why Job said, *The thing I feared has come upon me*. Think good and good follows.

14. Look at your fears; hold them up to the light of reason. Learn to laugh at your fears. That is the best medicine. Nothing can disturb you but your own thought. The

suggestions, statements, or threats of other persons have no power. The power is within you, and when your thoughts are focused on that which is good, then God's power is with your thoughts of good.

15. There is only one creative power, and it moves as harmony. There are no divisions or quarrels in it. Its source is love. This is why God's power is with your thoughts of good.

The great law of substitution is the answer to fear. Whatever you fear has its solution in the form of your desire. If you are sick, you desire health. If you are in the prison of fear, you desire freedom. Expect the good. Mentally concentrate on the good, and know that your subconscious mind answers you always. It never fails.

Chapter Twenty

How to Stay Young
in Spirit Forever

Your subconscious mind never grows old. It is timeless, ageless, and endless. It is a part of the universal mind of God, which was never born and will never die.

Fatigue or old age does not have an impact on any spiritual quality or power. Patience, kindness, veracity, humility, goodwill, peace, harmony, and brotherly love are attributes and qualities that never grow old. If you continue to generate these qualities here on this plane of life, you will always remain young in spirit.

Years alone are not responsible for bringing about degenerative disorders. It is not time itself, but the fear of time that has a harmful aging effect on our minds and bodies. Indeed, the neurotic fear of the effects of time may well be the cause of premature aging.

During the many years of my public life, I have had occasion to study the biographies of famous men and women who have continued their productive activities into the years well beyond the normal span of life. Some of them even achieve their greatness for the first time in old age. It has also been my privilege to meet and get to know countless individuals of no special prominence who, in their lesser sphere, belong among those hardy mortals who have proved that old age itself does not destroy the creative powers of the mind and body.

He Had Grown Old in His Thought Life

A few years ago I called on an old friend in London, England. He had recently turned eighty. For many people, this is a cause for rejoicing, but unfortunately not for him. I was deeply shocked when I saw him. He looked and felt weak, even ill, although he admitted that his doctor had not found any particular medical problem.

"Doctors are idiots," he proclaimed. "I know very well what my disease is. It is life itself."

I asked him what he meant.

"No one wants or needs me," he cried. "And why should they? I'm of no use to anyone. We are born, we grow up. We get old and we die, and that's the end of the story."

I saw that, in a way, he was right in his understanding of his illness. He was sick, not because of life, but because of the way he *viewed* life. His mental attitude of futility and worthlessness had brought about his sickness. He was looking forward only to senescence, and after that—nothing. Indeed, he had grown old in his thought life, and his subconscious mind made manifest everything he was expecting and dreading.

Age Is the Dawn of Wisdom

Unfortunately, many people have the same attitude as this unhappy man. They are afraid of what they term "old age," the end, and extinction. What this really means is that they are afraid of life. Yet life is endless. Age is not the flight of years, but the dawn of wisdom.

Wisdom is the awareness of the tremendous spiritual powers in your subconscious mind and the knowledge of how to apply these powers to lead a full and happy life. Get it out of your head once and for all that sixty-five, seventy-five, or eighty-five years of age is synonymous with the end for you or anybody else. It can be the beginning of a glorious, fruitful, active, and most productive life pattern, better than you have ever experienced. Believe this, expect it, and your subconscious will bring it to pass.

Welcome the Change

Old age is not a tragic occurrence. What we call the aging process is really change. It is to be welcomed joyfully and gladly. Each phase of human life is a step forward on a path that has no end. We have enormous powers that transcend the limits of our bodily powers. We have marvelous senses that transcend the limits of our five physical senses.

Life is spiritual and eternal. We need never grow old, for life, or God, cannot grow old. The Bible says that God is life. Life is self-renewing, eternal, indestructible, and is the reality of all people.

Life Is

A woman once asked Thomas Edison, the electrical wizard, "Mr. Edison, what is electricity?"

He replied, "Madame, electricity is. *Use* it."

Electricity is the name we give an invisible power that we do not fully comprehend. Yet we learn all we can about the principles of electricity and its uses. We use it in countless ways.

Scientists cannot see an electron with their eyes, yet they accept it as a scientific fact, because it is the only valid conclusion that coincides with other experimental evidence. We cannot see life. However, we know we are alive. Life is, and we are here to express it in all its beauty and glory.

Mind and Spirit Do Not Grow Old

This is eternal life: to know thee who alone art truly God. (John 17:3)

Anyone who thinks or believes that the earthly cycle of birth, adolescence, youth, maturity, and old age is all there is to life is indeed to be pitied. Such a person has no anchor, no hope, no vision. To that person life has no meaning.

This type of belief brings frustration, stagnation, cynicism, and a sense of hopelessness that leads to neurosis and mental aberrations of all kinds. What if you can no longer play a fast game of tennis or swim as fast as your children? What if your body has slowed down, or you walk with a slow step? Remember, life is always clothing itself anew. What people call death is but a journey to a new city in another dimension of life.

I say to those who come to my lectures that they should accept what we call *old age* gracefully. Age has its own glory, beauty, and wisdom that belong to it. Peace, love, joy, beauty, happiness, wisdom, goodwill, and understanding are qualities that never grow old or die.

Ralph Waldo Emerson, poet and philosopher, said, "We do not count a man's years until he has nothing else to count."

Your character, the quality of your mind, your faith, and your convictions are not subject to decay.

You Are as Young as You Think You Are

Following one of the lectures that I gave in London, England, a local surgeon told me, "I am eighty-four years of age, I operate every morning, visit patients in the afternoons, and I write for medical and other scientific journals in the evening."

His attitude was that he was as useful as he believed himself to be and as young as his thoughts. He continued, "It's true what you said. A person is as strong as he thinks he is, and as valuable as he thinks he is."

This surgeon has not surrendered to advancing years. He knows that he is immortal. "If I should pass on tomorrow," he said, "I will find myself helping and curing people in the next dimension, not with a surgeon's scalpel, but with mental and spiritual surgery."

Your Age Is an Asset

Don't ever walk away from an opportunity while thinking, "I'm too old to take this on," which is surely the way to stagnation and mental death. If you become convinced you are finished, your subconscious mind will accept that belief and bring it into reality. Some people are old at thirty, while others are young at eighty. The mind is the master weaver, the architect, the designer, and the sculptor. The playwright George Bernard Shaw was still active at ninety, and the artistic quality of his mind had not relaxed from active duty.

I meet men and women who tell me that some employers almost slam the door in their faces when they say they are over forty. This attitude on the part of employers is cold, callous, and completely void of compassion and understanding.

Who decreed that you must be under thirty-five years of age

to receive consideration? The reasoning behind this is shallow and specious. If the employer would stop to think, he or she would realize that the person was not selling his or her age or gray hair. Rather, the person would be willing to give of his or her talents, experience, and wisdom gathered through years of experience in the marketplace of life.

Your age should be a distinct asset to any organization, because of your practice and application through the years of the principles of the Golden Rule and the law of love and goodwill. Your gray hair, if you have any, should stand for greater wisdom, skill, and understanding. Your emotional and spiritual maturity should be a tremendous blessing to any organization.

People should not be shunted to the sidelines at sixty-five, or at any particular chronological age. That is a time of life when they could be most useful in handling personnel problems, making plans for the future, making decisions, and guiding others in the realm of creative ideas based on their experience and insight into the nature of the business.

Be Your Age

"I've had it with this business!" a Hollywood scriptwriter told me. "I've done first-rate work for years. I know my craft as well as anyone in town. I've won awards at festivals around the world."

Puzzled, I asked, "Then what's wrong?"

He threw up his hands. "The last story conference I went to, this thirty-year-old studio executive told me I couldn't relate to today's audiences. When I tried to argue, he informed me that he didn't want any scripts that weren't geared to the minds and tastes of boys twelve to eighteen! I walked out."

This is a tragic state of affairs. How are the great masses of people expected to become emotionally and spiritually mature if they are fed such a diet? They are being blinded to the potential they have within them for personal growth. They are told that they must glorify youth, even though in reality youth stands for inexperience, lack of discernment, and hasty judgment.

I Can Keep Up with the Best of Them

I know dozens of people in their sixties and older who spend their time in a frantic campaign to stay young. They take fad drugs, follow fad diets, waste their money on flimsy exercise machines whose virtues are touted on late-night television. Those with greater resources go in for spa treatments, liposuction, and cosmetic surgery. Their constant, futile cry is "Look, I can keep up with the best of them!"

Diets, multivitamins, and supports of all kinds will not keep these people young. They must realize that they grow old or remain young in accordance with their processes of thinking. Your subconscious mind is conditioned by your thoughts. If your thoughts are constantly on the beautiful, the noble, and the good, you will remain spiritually young regardless of your chronological years.

Fear of Aging

Job said, *The thing which I greatly feared is come upon me.* Many people fear old age. They are uncertain about the future, because they anticipate mental and physical deterioration as the years advance. What they think and feel comes to pass.

You grow old when you lose interest in life, when you cease to dream, to hunger after new truths, and to search for new worlds to conquer. When your mind is open to new ideas and new interests and when you raise the curtain and let in the sunshine and inspiration of new truths of life and the universe, you will be young and vital.

You Have Much to Give

Whether you are sixty-five or ninety-five years of age, you must realize you have much to give. You can help stabilize, advise, and direct the younger generation. You can give the benefit of your knowledge, your experience, and your wisdom. You can always look ahead, for at all times you are gazing into infinite life. You will find that you can never cease to unveil the glories and wonders of life. Try to learn something new every moment of the day and you will find your mind will always be young.

Growing Old with Gladness

While lecturing in India, I was introduced to a man whose friends told me was one hundred ten years old. He had the most beautiful face I have ever seen. He seemed transfigured by the radiance of an inner light. There was a rare beauty in his eyes. I could see he had grown old in years with gladness and with no indication that his mind had dimmed its lights.

Retirement—A New Adventure

Be sure that your mind never retires. Your mind must be like a parachute—it's of no use at all unless it opens up. Be open and receptive to new ideas. I have seen people of sixty-five and seventy retire. They seemed to rot away, and in a few months passed on. They obviously felt that their life had come to an end, and because they thought so, it *was* so.

Retirement can be a new venture, a new challenge, a new path, the beginning of the fulfillment of a long dream. It is inexpressibly depressing to hear someone say, "What will I do now that I am retired?" He or she is saying, in effect, "I am mentally and physically dead. My mind is bankrupt of ideas."

All this is a false picture. The real truth is that you can accomplish more at ninety than you did at sixty, because each day you are growing in wisdom and understanding of life and the universe through your new studies and interest.

Instead of saying, "I am old," say, "I am wise in the way of the Divine life." Don't let the corporation, newspapers, or statistics hold a picture before you of old age, declining years, decrepitude, senility, and uselessness. Reject it, for it is a lie. Refuse to be hypnotized by such propaganda. Affirm life—not death. Get a vision of yourself as happy, radiant, successful, serene, and powerful.

Accept what we call old age gracefully. Age has its own glory, beauty, and wisdom that belong to it. Peace, love, joy, beauty, happiness, wisdom, goodwill, and understanding are qualities that never grow old or die.

Retirement can be a new venture, a new challenge, a new path, the beginning of the fulfillment of a long dream.

Graduating to a Better Job

Frank W., an acquaintance, was forced out of his job. The company told him it was because of a new restructuring plan, but he believed his age of sixty-five lay behind the decision.

"Do you feel bitter about being the victim of discrimination?" I asked him. "Are you going to sue?"

He laughed ruefully. "I could, I suppose. And I guess I might very well win in court. But why should I spend my time and energy that way? I haven't lost my job, the company has lost my services."

He paused, then added, "The way I look at it, I just got my promotion from kindergarten to the first grade."

"How do you mean?"

"Well, for instance," he replied, "when I graduated from high school, I climbed to the next rung of the ladder by going to college. I took a step forward in my education and understanding of life in general. My career was another step, or maybe a few steps. Now I've been liberated to do things I've always wanted to do. In other words, being let go is still another step upward on the ladder of life."

Frank came to the wise conclusion that he was no longer going to concentrate on making a living. Now he was going to give all his attention to living life. He had been a passionate amateur photographer for years. He made a commitment to take courses in photographic technique at a nearby art institute. Later he went on a voyage around the world. At each place he visited, he took dozens of rolls of film. He now lectures before various groups, lodges, and clubs and is in constant demand.

There are countless ways of taking an interest in something worthwhile outside yourself. Become enthusiastic over new creative ideas, make spiritual progress, and continue to learn and to grow. In this manner you remain young in heart, because you are hungering and thirsting after new truths, and your body will reflect your thinking at all times.

Be a Producer, Not a Prisoner

Laws that prohibit employers from discriminating against men and women because of age are a step in the right direction, but laws alone cannot alter the way people think. Someone of sixty-five years may be younger mentally, physically, and physiologically than many people of thirty. We are here to enjoy the fruits of our labor, to be a producer and not a prisoner of society that sentences us to idleness because of our age.

A person's body slows down gradually as he or she advances through the years, but his conscious mind can be made much more active, alert, alive, and quickened by the inspiration from his or her subconscious mind. The mind, in reality, never grows old. Job said,

> If I could only go back to the old days, to the time when God was watching over me, when his lamp shone above my head, and by its light I walked through darkness! If I could be as in the days of my prime, when God protected my home. (Job 29:2–4)

The Secret of Youth

To recapture the days of your youth, feel the miraculous, healing, self-renewing power of your subconscious mind moving through your whole being. Know and feel that you are inspired, lifted up, rejuvenated, revitalized, and recharged spiritually. You can bubble over with enthusiasm and joy, as in the days of your youth, for the simple reason that you can always mentally and emotionally recapture that joyous state.

The candle that shines upon your head is Divine Intelligence. It reveals to you everything you need to know. It enables you to affirm the presence of your good, regardless of appearances. You walk by the guidance of your subconscious mind, because you know that the dawn appears and the shadows flee.

Get a Vision

Instead of saying, "I am old," say, "I am wise in the way of the Divine life." Don't let the corporation, newspapers, or statistics hold a picture before you of old age, declining years, decrepitude, senility, and uselessness. Reject it, for it is a lie. Refuse to be hypnotized by such propaganda. Affirm life—not death. Get a vision of yourself as happy, radiant, successful, serene, and powerful.

Your Mind Does Not Grow Old

The pioneering heart surgeon Michael DeBakey developed the first roller pump for blood in 1932. At the age of ninety, Dr. DeBakey got permission to start clinical trials on a new invention, a tiny pump that can be implanted in the chests of those with severe heart disease. Not content with research, DeBakey pursued an active surgical schedule as well. A colleague said, "It would take other people five or six lifetimes to do what he's done."

DeBakey summed up his philosophy at ninety this way: "As long as you have challenges and are physically and mentally able, life is stimulating and invigorating."

As Old as You Think and Feel

My father learned the French language at sixty-five years of age and became an authority on it at seventy. He began the study of Gaelic when he was over sixty and became an acknowledged and famous teacher of the subject. He assisted my sister at an institute of higher education until he passed away at ninety-nine. His mind was as clear at ninety-nine as it had been when he was twenty. In fact, his reasoning powers became even sharper with age. Truly, you are as old as you think and feel.

We Need Our Senior Citizens

Marcus Porcius Cato, the Roman patriot, learned Greek at eighty. Madame Ernestine Schumann-Heink, the great German-American contralto, reached the pinnacle of her musical success after she became a grandmother.

The Greek philosopher Socrates learned to play musical instruments when he was eighty years old. Michelangelo was painting his greatest canvases at eighty. At eighty, Cios Simonides won the prize for poetry, Johann von Goethe finished *Faust*, and Leopold von Ranke commenced his *History of the World*, which he finished at ninety-two.

Alfred, Lord Tennyson wrote a magnificent poem, "Crossing the Bar," at eighty-three. Isaac Newton was hard at work close to eighty-five. At eighty-eight John Wesley was directing, preaching, and guiding Methodism.

Jeanne Louise Calment of Arles, France, was not famous as these people were famous. In her youth, she once met a famous man, the painter Vincent van Gogh, but that did not bring her any particular notice. It was not until after her one hundredth birthday that those around her began to pay attention. For her, it was the occasion to give up riding her bicycle every day!

On Calment's 110th birthday, she received greetings and good wishes from around the world. Her 118th birthday made her the oldest documented human in history. When asked how she had done it, she said, "I took pleasure when I could. I acted clearly and morally and without regret. I'm very lucky." At 122, her smile was as radiant and contagious as ever.

Let us place our senior citizens in high places and give them every opportunity to bring forth the flowers of Paradise.

If you are retired, get interested in the laws of life and the wonders of your subconscious mind. Do something you have always wanted to do. Study new subjects and investigate new ideas.

As a hind longs for the running streams, so do I long for thee, O, God. With my whole being I thirst for God, the living God. (Psalm 42:1)

The Fruits of Old Age

*That man will grow sturdier than he was in youth, he
will return to the days of his prime.* (Job 33:25)

Old age really means the contemplation of the truths of God
from the highest standpoint. Realize that you are on an endless
journey, a series of important steps in the ceaseless, tireless,
endless ocean of life. Then, with the psalmist you will say,

*[They are] vigorous in old age like trees full of sap,
luxuriant, wide-spreading.* (Psalm 92:14)

*But the harvest of the Spirit is love, joy, peace, patience,
kindness, goodness, fidelity, gentleness, and self-
control. There is no law dealing with such things as
these.* (Galatians 5:22–23)

You are a child of infinite life, which knows no end, and you
are an heir to eternity.

IDEAS TO REMEMBER

1. Patience, kindness, love, goodwill, joy, happiness, wisdom, and understanding are qualities that never grow
   old. Cultivate them and express them and remain young
   in mind and body.

2. The neurotic fear of the effects of time may well be the
   cause of premature aging.

3. Age is not the flight of years; it is the dawn of wisdom in
   the mind of humans.

4. The most productive years of your life can be from sixty-five to ninety-five.

5. Welcome the advancing years. It means you are moving higher on the path of life, which has no end.

6. God is life, and that is your life now. Life is self-renewing, eternal, and indestructible and is the reality of all humans. You live forever, because your life is God's life.

7. You cannot see your mind, but you know you have a mind. You cannot see spirit, but you know that the spirit of the game, the spirit of the artist, the spirit of the musician, and the spirit of the speaker is real. Likewise, the spirit of goodness, truth, and beauty moving in your mind and heart are real. You cannot see life, but you know you are alive.

8. Old age may be called the contemplation of the truths of God from the highest standpoint. The joys of old age are greater than those of youth. Your mind is engaged in spiritual and mental athletics. Nature slows your body so that you may have the opportunity to meditate on things divine.

9. We do not count a man's years until he has nothing else to count. Your faith and convictions are not subject to decay.

10. You are as young as you think you are. You are as strong as you think you are. You are as useful as you think you are. You are as young as your thoughts.

11. Your gray hairs are an asset. You are not selling your

gray hairs. You are selling your talent, abilities, and wisdom that you have garnered through the years.

12. Fad diets and expensive pills won't keep you young. *As a man thinks, so is he.*

13. Fear of old age can bring about physical and mental deterioration. *The thing I greatly feared has come upon me.*

14. You grow old when you cease to dream and when you lose interest in life. You grow old if you are irritable, crotchety, petulant, and cantankerous. Fill your mind with the truths of God and radiate the sunshine of his love—this is youth.

15. Look ahead, for at all times you are gazing into infinite life.

16. Your retirement is a new venture. Take up new studies and interests. You can do the things you always wanted to do when you were so busy making a living. Give your attention to living life.

17. Become a producer and not a prisoner of society. Don't hide your light under a bushel.

18. The secret of youth is love, joy, inner peace, and laughter. In God there is fullness of joy. In God there is no darkness at all.

19. You are needed. Some of the great philosophers, artists, scientists, writers, and others accomplished their greatest work after they were eighty years old.

20. The fruits of old age are love, joy, peace, patience, gentleness, goodness, faith, meekness, and temperance.

21. You are a child of the infinite life that knows no end.
    You are an heir to eternity. You are wonderful!

Old age is not a tragic occurrence. What we call the aging process is really change. Each phase of human life is a step forward on a path that has no end. We have enormous powers that transcend the limits of our bodily powers. We have marvelous senses that transcend the limits of our five physical senses. Life is spiritual and eternal.

Index

About the Author

Joseph Murphy, born on May 20, 1898, in a small town in the County of Cork, Ireland, was enrolled in the National School, where he excelled. Encouraged to study for the priesthood, he was accepted as a Jesuit seminarian.

However, by the time he reached his late teen years, he began to question the Catholic orthodoxy of the Jesuits and he withdrew from the seminary. As his goal was to explore new ideas and gain new experiences, a goal he could not pursue in Catholic-dominated Ireland, he left his family to go to America.

He arrived at the Ellis Island Immigration Center with only five dollars in his pocket. His first project was to find a place to live. He was fortunate to locate a rooming house where he shared a room with a pharmacist who worked in a local drugstore.

His knowledge of English was minimal as Gaelic was spoken both in his home and at school, so like most Irish immigrants, Murphy worked as a day laborer, earning enough to keep fed and housed.

He and his roommate became good friends, and when a job opened up at the drugstore where his friend worked, Murphy was hired to be an assistant to the pharmacist. He immediately enrolled in a school to study pharmacy, and qualified as a full-fledged pharmacist. He eventually purchased the drugstore and for the next few years ran a successful business.

When the United States entered World War II, Murphy enlisted in the U.S. Army and was assigned to work as a pharmacist in a medical unit. While in the army, he renewed his interest in religion and began to read extensively about various religious beliefs. After his discharge, he chose not to return to his career in pharmacy. He traveled extensively and took courses in several universities both in the United States and abroad.

From his studies, he became enraptured by the various Asian religions and went to India to learn about them in depth. He extended his studies to the great philosophers from ancient times until the present.

The one person who most influenced Murphy was Dr. Thomas Troward, who was a judge as well as a philosopher, doctor, and professor. Judge Troward became Joseph's mentor. From him he not only learned philosophy, theology, and law but also was introduced to mysticism and particularly to the Masonic order. Murphy became an active member of this order and over the years rose in the Masonic ranks to the 32nd degree in the Scottish Rite.

Upon his return to the United States, he chose to become a minister. As his concept of Christianity was not traditional and indeed ran counter to most of the Christian denominations, he founded his own church in Los Angeles. He attracted a small number of congregants, but it did not take long for his message of optimism and hope to attract many men and women to his church.

Dr. Murphy was a proponent of the New Thought movement, which advocated combining a metaphysical, spiritual, and pragmatic approach to the way we think and live, to uncover the secret of attaining what we truly desire. We can do all these things only as we have found the law and worked out the understanding of the law, which God seemed to have written in riddles in the past.

Over the years other churches joined with Dr. Murphy in developing an organization called the Divine Science Federation, which acts as an umbrella for all Divine Science Churches.

Murphy's local Church of Divine Science grew so large that he had to rent the Wilshire Ebell Theater, a former movie house. His services were so well attended that even this venue could not always accommodate all who wished to attend. To reach the vast numbers of people who wanted to hear his message, Dr. Murphy created a weekly radio talk show, which eventually reached an audience of more than a million listeners.

He taped his lectures and radio programs, and the initial success that he saw in marketing the cassettes started a new venture to increase his outreach. Tapes featured lectures explaining biblical texts, and provided meditations and prayers for his listeners. He also started to publish pamphlets and small books of his inspirational material.

As a result of his books, tapes, and radio broadcasts, Dr. Murphy's reputation grew exponentially and he was invited to lecture throughout the United States, Europe, and Asia. In addition to religious matters, he spoke on the historical values of life, on the art of wholesome living, and on the teachings of great philosophers—from both the Western and Asian cultures. In all his lectures, he emphasized the importance of understanding the power of the subconscious mind and the life-principles based on belief in the one God, the "I AM."

He wrote more than thirty books. This book, *The Power of Your Subconscious Mind*, first published in 1963, became an immediate bestseller. Millions of copies have been sold and continue to be sold all over the world in a wide variety of languages.

Dr. Murphy died in December 1981. His wife, Dr. Jean Murphy, continued his ministry until her death.